Self Love & Confidence Workbook for Strong Women Use the Power of Positive Thinking to Find Your Worth! 2 in 1

A 10 week program to build self esteem with daily Affirmations, Guided Meditations & Hypnosis

Written by: Elena Wright, Brandy Wells

Elena Wright © Copyright 2020 - All rights reserved.

The content contained within this book may not be reproduced, duplicated or transmitted without direct written permission from the author or the publisher.

Under no circumstances will any blame or legal responsibility be held against the publisher, or author, for any damages, reparation, or monetary loss due to the information contained within this book, either directly or indirectly.

Image: Freepick.com. This cover has been designed using resources from Freepick.com

Legal Notice:

This book is copyright protected. It is only for personal use. You cannot amend, distribute, sell, use, quote or paraphrase any part, or the content within this book, without the consent of the author or publisher.

Disclaimer Notice:

Please note the information contained within this document is for educational and entertainment purposes only. All effort has been executed to present accurate, up to date, reliable, complete information. No warranties of any kind are declared or implied. Readers acknowledge that the author is not engaging in the rendering of legal, financial, medical or professional advice. The content within this book has been derived from various sources. Please consult a licensed professional before attempting any techniques outlined in this book.

By reading this document, the reader agrees that under no circumstances is the author responsible for any losses, direct or indirect, that are incurred as a result of the use of information contained within this document, including, but not limited to, errors, omissions, or inaccuracies.

Self-Love for the Feminine Soul

Daily Affirmations, Guided Meditations, and Hypnosis for Healing Your Body and Mind

A 10 Week Program packed with activities to guide you to Self-Love

Written by: Elena Wright, Brandy Wells

"And the world cannot be discovered by a journey of miles, no matter how long, but only by a spiritual journey, a journey of one inch, very arduous and humbling and joyful, by which we arrive at the ground at our own feet, and learn to be at home."

Wendell Berry (*The Unforeseen Wilderness*, 1971)[1]

Table of Contents

Note from the Authors 11

Introduction 17
    The Roots of Self-Love 19
    But Wait, What is Self-Love? 20
    Let's Explore Femininity 22
    Why Begin This Process? 24
    How to Use This Book 26
    A Guide to Self-Hypnosis 27
    Self-Love for the Feminine Soul: A Promise 29

Chapter 1 - Meet Yourself Where You Are, Right Now 31
    Exhale the Past 36
    Release the Future 37
    Accept the Present 38
    Week One Daily Affirmations 39
    Week One Healing Activities 40
    Week One Reflection 45

Chapter 2 - The First Steps Toward Self-Love 47
    Is This When We Start the Bubble Baths and Manicures? 50
    From Punishment to Praise 52
    Take Care of Yourself 54
    Laugh a Little 54
    Week 2 Daily Affirmations 56
    Week 2 Healing Activities 57

Week 2 Reflection 61

Chapter 3 - Embrace the Vulnerability of Self-Care..63
Getting Comfortable with Vulnerability...65
The Vulnerability of Self-Care 68
Making Self-Care Tangible 71
Week 3 Daily Affirmations 73
Week 3 Healing Activities 74
Week 3 Reflection 78

Chapter 4 - Dive Deep to Learn Your Authentic Truth..79
Dig into Your Emotional Tendencies 81
Be Patient with Difficult Emotions 84
Honor Your Authentic Self 86
Week 4 Daily Affirmations 88
Week 4 Healing Activities 89
Week 4 Reflection 93

Chapter 5 - Cultivate Undeniable Self-Trust 95
Feel Confident in Belonging to Yourself 97
Acknowledge Your Strengths 102
Be Realistic and Follow Through..103
Week 5 Daily Affirmations 105
Week 5 Healing Activities 106
Week 5 Reflection 110

Chapter 6 - Protect Your Energy to Find Balance Between Rest and Activity 111
Self-Neglect in Action...113
Rest to Transform 117

Finding Ease in Your Activities 119
Week 6 Daily Affirmations 120
Week 6 Healing Activities 122
Week 6 Reflection 126

Chapter 7 - Create an Inner Voice of Kindness and Compassion 127

Make Peace With Your Inner Voice 130
Shifting Toward Compassion 132
Build a Flow of Kindness 135
Week 7 Daily Affirmations 136
Week 7 Healing Activities 137
Week 7 Reflection 141

Chapter 8 - Build a Self-Image of Strength and Resilience 143

What is Your Self-Image? 146
Restore Connections by Finding an Inner Friend 149
The Courage to Rewrite Your Self-Image 152
Week 8 Daily Affirmations 154
Week 8 Healing Activities 156
Week 8 Reflection 160

Chapter 9 - Celebrate Your Efforts and Bask in the Small Successes 161

True Self-Celebration 163
The Little Things Are the Big Things 166
Make it a Habit! 168
Small Steps, Big Impact 171
Week 9 Daily Affirmations 172

Week 9 Healing Activities 174
Week 9 Reflection 177

Chapter 10 - Breathe Self-Love into Your Routines Moving Forward 179

Explore Your Routines 181
Weave an Element of Self-Love 183
Acknowledge the Role of Society 188
Check in and Maintain Your Efforts 189
Week 10 Daily Affirmations 191
Week 10 Healing Activities 192
Week 10 Reflection 196

Conclusion: Tying it All Together 197

Revisiting Our Promises 199
Self-Love, Now 201
Let the Feminine Be 202
Where to Go From Here 203
Ending with a Promise 205

Resources 207

Note from the Authors

Self-love can be a difficult topic to get on board with. Believe me, I get that more than anyone. My journey with self-love began as an inner battle. I had been struggling with my mental health and confidence, and felt so much resistance toward myself. I was neglecting my inner self and forcing my outer self to behave in ways that didn't align with my true values. I was rejecting myself, judging myself harshly, and generally making life harder than it needed to be. Despite this extreme resistance, I knew something needed to change. I slowly started trying out different practices that settled my nervous system, brought me out of my head, and helped me find presence in my body. I started to see these practices as tools I could employ throughout the day to offer myself a bit of care, and begin to calm the inner critic.

The activities in this book are a mix of a few of the tools I've found most helpful in cultivating a consistent self-love practice. Affirmations, hypnosis, guided meditations, journal prompts, light physical activity, and clear visuals have all helped me find achievable ways to nurture myself, and work toward trusting myself again. Your toolbox will inevitably be unique to you, but I hope the provided activities will at least spark your curiosity, and encourage you to explore the possibilities for your own self-love practice.

I've chosen to incorporate this idea of the feminine soul because I've noticed some patterns between my own self-judgment and how society says we need to be as humans. Often, we are taught to reject certain sides of ourselves. Regardless of how we identify, we all possess some form of feminine energy, but something tells us we should hide these aspects of ourselves. Over time, I learned to be afraid of being vulnerable around friends. I started to hide my emotions and true feelings at work. I learned to use my generosity and nurturing qualities exclusively for pleasing others. I learned that only certain people are allowed to access femininity, and even then, it is only acceptable in certain situations.

I also noticed that the people in my life who come off as the most confident, brave, and joyful, are people who embrace their feminine energy. They express themselves freely, aren't afraid to discuss their true feelings, and don't let society dictate which parts of themselves they can reveal. They are the folks who embrace themselves fully in every setting, and never leave parts of themselves behind in order to fit in, please others, or edit themselves into a certain role. I feel that many of us keep certain aspects of ourselves hidden for fear of being perceived as weak, dramatic, emotional, or simply "too much." And frankly, I don't want to live like that anymore. I see embracing my feminine energy, and embracing my whole self, as an act of courage. I see it as a brave and necessary first step, a radical access point for building real self-love.

As you read the book, you'll see that I don't view self-love in quite the same way that it often gets portrayed. I don't believe we have to love ourselves before we can be loved by others. I know that self-love can be more challenging for some of us than others, because it was, and still often is, challenging for me. But that doesn't mean we have to wait until we get there in order to receive any love at all.

I think the whole point of self-love is learning that we are all deserving of love *now*. We can receive love in our lives, while also working toward loving ourselves better. It shouldn't have to be all or nothing. I also don't see self-love as this one-time, "achieve it, earn a trophy, and you are healed forever" thing. To me, self-love is a verb. An ongoing and necessary action, like exercising and nourishing our bodies, that we should practice every day of our lives.

My idea is, self-love comes in little gestures and steps that we carry out each day. We are all worthy of it now, and we can all achieve it if we just listen to our own needs.

If this is the first of our books you've read, please consider checking out *Hello, it's Confidence Calling* and *Modern Mindfulness*! *Hello, it's Confidence Calling* pairs well with this book, as many people exploring self-love also yearn for more confidence in their lives. Self-love starts as an internal shift, and cultivating more confidence is a way to bring the practice outward and into other areas of your life. Mindfulness is another excellent tool to employ in your self-love practice, as shifting your focus to the present helps remind you to be gentle with yourself in your thoughts and actions. We are continually creating new books to help our readers understand themselves better and cultivate an even better relationship with themselves.

Thank you for purchasing this book. Our readers are important to us, and we would love to hear from each of you. Please leave us a review to let us know what you think of our books, and share them with your friends!

Thank you for the support, and I sincerely hope you enjoy this exploration of self-love.

Disclaimer: Please note that the information provided in this book is for entertainment purposes only. The writings within this text are the opinions and advice of the authors, and we have made every effort to present accurate, reliable, and up to date information. No warranties of any kind are declared or implied. Readers acknowledge that the authors are not engaging in the rendering of legal, financial, medical, or professional advice. Please consult a licensed professional before attempting any techniques outlined in this book. Do not attempt any meditation or hypnosis exercises while driving or operating machinery. The advice provided in this book is not meant to precede or replace help from a medical or mental health professional.

Introduction

The concept of self-love has earned quite a bit of hype in recent years. Most of us are likely familiar with this idea that loving yourself should come first. It's that whole notion of putting on your own oxygen mask before assisting others. You have to love yourself before you can expect love in return, right?

Well, honestly, this common spin on self-love doesn't quite sit right with me.

For some of us, self-love doesn't come so easily.

Influencers and gurus spouting claims that self-love is the only ingredient missing from your life may bring up feelings of shame. If fear and shame control our thoughts on this topic, a lack of self-love may feel like yet another thing we are failing to achieve. And the notion that we are not loveable until we have learned to fully love ourselves is not only depressing, but harmfully inaccurate.

You deserve love and *are* loved, regardless of your current relationship with yourself. Even if you don't understand how to arrive at self-love, it is an important first step to acknowledge that you are already loveable, right now.

Yes, self-love is certainly a worthy goal, but my thought is that guilt-tripping ourselves may not be the best way to get there.

The Roots of Self-Love

Self-love is similar to happiness in some ways. They're both words we weigh down with endless expectations. They're also words we tend to place in the future.

"I will be happy when I earn X amount of money, when I pay off my debt, when I get my next big project done, or when I move into a new house."

"I will love myself when I get that promotion I have been waiting for, when my body looks how I want it to, when I find my dream partner, or when I kick the bad habit I've tried to beat forever."

Does any of this sound familiar?

Here's a bit of good news and bad news. Nothing outside of yourself is the ticket to achieving self-love. This means the roots of self-love are already inside of you, right now. This also means you can't expect changing your body, your job, your partner, or your address to automatically fill you with the love and happiness you seek.

But let's kick the guilt, shame, and fear to the curb before they have a chance to take over here. Self-love can be difficult. And it's especially difficult when society teaches us that our lives need to be perfect and also effortless. We need to be easygoing and down-to-earth, but also on top of every tiny detail of our lives. When these thoughts make up your mental dialogue, do you see how failure would be so much easier than success? Do you see how self-critique would be so much easier than self-love?

So let's adjust our expectations. Let's discover the roots of self-love inside of us, and rewrite a more realistic internal dialogue that helps them flourish and thrive.

But Wait, What *is* Self-Love?

If self-love isn't this impossible yet effortless thing we are all struggling to understand, how can we redefine it in a way that might provide relief rather than anxiety?

My definition is below; however, I encourage you to pause here and write out a definition of the kind of self-love you are striving for.

One of the most important things to realize is that this process will be different for everyone. You can take bits and pieces from this book and apply them to your experience, but ultimately, your experience is yours. Each piece, including your definition of self-love, should be crafted with language that resonates best for you.

My definition of self-love is nurturing and accepting yourself in the present moment, despite any urge to lean into shame, guilt, or fear. It is the act of continuing to stand up for yourself in this way over and over again, no matter how tempted you are to critique your own flaws. Self-love is not a state of eternal bliss that we arrive at one day. It is instead a repeated action. It is cultivating a toolbelt filled with steps you can take to accept your limitations, provide yourself space for expression and healing, and create more ease surrounding any difficulty you may be facing.

If you feel very far away from this definition, know that this is perfectly normal. So many of us struggle to love ourselves each day. This is because we have learned that paying more attention to our fears and flaws will keep us safe. Our fears tell us that we are lacking in some way, and every time we listen to that, we reinforce and strengthen this negative thought pattern.

Relax in your seat a bit. Fear doesn't get to take the driver's seat here. You've got the steering wheel. Turning inward, getting curious, and defining your own brand of self-love will help you build confidence and make the changes you've always wanted for yourself. Instead of seeing the process as slow and arduous, what if you tried to see it as luxurious and indulgent? Can you see the time spent as playful, fruitful, and inarguably necessary for your own healing? Bear with me.

Let's Explore Femininity

So we've begun to understand a bit more about self-love, but what about this concept of the feminine soul?

Self-love, and love in general, tend to be concepts we consider feminine in some way. I'd like to break up the notion that these ideas can only apply to a certain group of people. Every human, regardless of identity, exhibits some feminine qualities. By feminine qualities, I mean a call to creativity, expressing emotions, deeply connecting with the people you love, or tapping into your intuition. We all have feminine properties, and tapping into that wise, soft, and playful side of ourselves can be an extremely vulnerable endeavor.

Fear tells us we have to see everything as black or white. Anxiety encourages us to jump to the worst-case scenario. Shame tells us that our flaws make us unloveable. By tapping into the feminine elements of who we are, we can fight back against these urges to harden and put up walls. We can explore the idea that staying soft is an even more courageous approach to life's difficult moments. We can take a less harsh, less rushed approach to problem-solving and be a bit kinder to ourselves during the process. Embracing the gentle ease to be found in our feminine sides is a worthy path toward self-love.

Why Begin This Process?

Beginning the steps toward self-love may feel futile and pointless, and believe me, I get it. Whether you have already tried other programs or strategies with no luck, or you're just exploring this topic for the first time, let's take a look at some of the benefits that may encourage you to keep going.

Benefits of Cultivating Self-Love:

- Stop letting guilt and shame limit your ability to show up fully in your life
- Stop mistaking shyness and rigidity for your personality
- Stop letting the walls you've put up prevent you from expressing yourself creatively and freely
- Connect with others more authentically

- Stop letting self-doubt and self-sabotage prevent you from going after what you want
- Start living a life free from the physical and mental side effects of self-doubt and self-loathing
- Start exuding confidence, humor, and ease and allowing them to override fearful behaviors
- Rewrite your negative thoughts to stop feeling trapped inside your mind
- Develop a better relationship with your mind, learning to view thoughts objectively without becoming attached to them or controlled by them
- Accept and nurture yourself despite any mistakes or flaws
- Become more resilient when you do experience negativity or failure
- Learn to trust yourself and your intuition
- Develop routines that feel achievable and healthy

Does this sound like what you've been wanting? Know that this is all achievable. But also know that you are worthy of self-love now, even before you've begun.

You were born worthy of love.

And if any part of you is resisting that sentence, take note. Take it as a sign to dig deeper.

How to Use This Book

This book is designed as a ten-week program packed with affirmations, meditations, hypnosis, and many other activities to guide you toward a place of self-love. Each chapter expands upon a specific topic, and the accompanying activities allow you to put what you've learned into practice. Each day you can use a new affirmation as a focal point to return to if you get distracted by negative thoughts.

The idea is to go through this book one day at a time for the full ten weeks. Each day you can simply journal about or meditate on one of the affirmations, or try out one of the guided activities. Feel free to go at your own pace and craft an experience that feels healing for you. This is your experience, and it is important that you feel capable of guiding yourself in the way that works best for you. Make sure to answer the reflection questions before moving on to the next chapter, and continue like this throughout the book.

A Guide to Self-Hypnosis

This aspect of the book may be new to you, but that's okay. We've worked in consultation with a certified hypnotherapist to create easy self-hypnosis activities you can do at home. All you will need is a device for recording your voice, and a quiet, comfortable place to listen to your recording. You will record yourself saying the provided hypnosis script slowly and clearly. You are welcome to make adjustments to the script to include elements that are specific to your life. Then, you will get comfortable, close your eyes, and listen to the recording in a relaxed state.

We've chosen to incorporate hypnotherapy into this book because it helps spark quick and lasting change. This works because the relaxed state you enter allows hypnosis to move past the "thinking brain" that may be tempted to judge or resist the situation. Accessing the subconscious from a relaxed, nonjudgmental state helps the message sink in and leave a lasting impact. The scripts we've included use neuro-linguistic programming to create potent guided hypnosis exercises that help you cultivate a better relationship with yourself.

The act of listening to your own voice is an exercise in bringing the outer and inner versions of yourself together in harmony. Guiding yourself to a better mental state will build lasting self-trust and remind you that your inner self needs consistent attention and care.

Disclaimer: Do not attempt any of the self-hypnosis or meditation activities in this book while driving or operating machinery. Consult your health practitioner or mental health professional before attempting self-hypnosis. These activities are for self-discovery purposes, and not meant to substitute professional help from certified medical or mental health practitioners.

Self-Love for the Feminine Soul: A Promise

No matter how you have arrived on this page, I am glad you are here. You've taken a step toward cultivating self-love in the form of small daily actions. The activities in this book are designed to nudge your mind, body, and nervous system into a softer, more relaxed state. This gentle approach to nurturing and healing your mind and body will chip away at the walls you've built up, and help you discover the roots of self-love you've had inside you all along. This is not an external search, but rather, an uncovering of a truth that has always been.

I encourage you to pause again here and write down one promise to yourself related to your journey toward practicing self-love. This promise can be big or small. What is important is your intention to keep it. Making and keeping this first promise will start the process of building the self-trust needed to practice self-love.

My promise to you is that if you begin this journey from a place of curiosity, kindness, and openness, you will trigger the shift necessary to build a self-love practice.

Here are a few promises you may consider making to yourself now:

- I promise to complete this book within ten weeks.
- I promise to complete this book within one year.
- I promise to meditate on one self-love affirmation each day for one week.
- I promise to read chapter 1 now.
- I promise to adjust my self-love practice daily as it feels appropriate for my body and mind.
- I promise to be a little bit kinder to myself today.
- I promise to do one thing right now that is self-loving

Once you've decided on your promise, flip the page to get started!

Chapter 1

Meet Yourself Where You Are, Right Now

"Yesterday is gone. Tomorrow has not yet come. We have only today. Let us begin."

Mother Teresa (Goodreads, 2020)[2]

Imagine you have a big presentation coming up at work. You know you have the skills to nail it, but you've struggled with public speaking in the past. Those past scenarios keep playing out in your mind, and you begin to imagine yourself failing at this task as well. In this scenario, you are unknowingly allowing mistakes from the past and uncertainty in the future to impact your confidence, performance, and preparation in the present.

Do you notice that past scenarios shape the way you view yourself in the present?

Do you allow your mind to come up with negative stories about the future that consume your thoughts?

Do you use situations in the past or future to justify why you are not good enough?

Do you see how these thought patterns rob you of the ability to feel confident and fully accept yourself in the present?

It's safe to say the subconscious tendency for the mind to gravitate toward the past or the future is natural.

Whether you are frequently frustrated by this tendency, or you are just becoming aware of it, know that you are not alone. Our minds learn to focus on the stuff we choose to feed them. If we feed our minds stories of mistakes from the past or predictions of coming up short in the future, our minds will get really good at seeing these storylines in every scenario of our lives. This includes a self-love practice.

Before diving into the journey of cultivating self-love, it is important to develop some awareness surrounding your inner dialogue, and your willingness to accept yourself as you are, right now. It's time to retrain the brain to recognize these storylines of the past and future without becoming attached to them or mistaking them for the truth. As the past is behind you and the future is still uncertain, the only point of access to really accept yourself, get to know yourself, and learn to love yourself, is by embracing yourself in the present.

So how does this look in action? If your storyline is that you are dreadful at public speaking, start by noticing when this thought comes up, and how it makes you feel. Notice how long you dwell on the thought and how much power you give it. Maybe you even notice that your body tenses up, your palms get clammy, or your heart begins to race when thinking about a negative past experience. Practice disrupting this storyline with a kind thought, or reframing it in a way that moves from critical to accepting.

Here are some examples of how you can try reframing a self-critical thought regarding the past or future. The goal is to shift into a place of self-acceptance that allows you to release storylines and meet yourself in the present moment.

Self-Critical, Past/Future-Oriented Thought	Self-Accepting, Present-Oriented Thought
"I will fail at my public speaking assignment because I failed in the past."	"I have the tools I need to perform at my best and succeed at the tasks I am given."
"I won't amount to anything in the future because I never follow through with my goals."	"I am learning the skills to create goals that feel realistic and achievable for me. I trust myself to take one small step every day."
"I have experienced negative treatment in relationships in the past because I am unworthy of love and joy."	"I have been hurt in the past, and I allow myself to acknowledge and heal that pain. I am worthy of experiencing healthy, profound love and joy."
"I won't develop a lasting self-love practice because I can't envision a future where I feel good about myself."	"I have struggled with self-love in the past because of certain factors in my life that are not my fault. I can cultivate self-love that meets me where I am each day."

As this is chapter 1, we are naturally at the starting point of this self-love exploration, right? Actually, we cannot begin if our minds are stuck in the past, or we've mentally raced off into the future. This week is all about self-acceptance, so let's take a second to notice and accept the mental space we are in. Let's clear away any storylines that may be getting in the way of fully settling into the present moment, here together on this page.

Exhale the Past

Repetitive thoughts of the past can be quite tormenting if we let them dominate our minds. Not only are they limiting us, but they can also be a serious distraction from our daily tasks. Let's use the analogy of driving down the highway. The rearview mirror is there for a reason and can inform your decisions in the present. However, you would never put all of your focus on what is happening behind you. Doing so would jeopardize your driving performance and needlessly add risk to the situation. This is similar to what happens if we allow thoughts of the past to take over our minds and guide our behavior in the present. See the past as a tool, as useful information, and loosen your grip on any unproductive storylines that feel self-critical.

Exhaling the past means removing one barrier that is preventing you from accessing self-love in the present. This is a practice that takes time, and the activities throughout this book will help you get a little bit better at identifying this pattern each time it comes up. Soon, exhaling the past will become second-nature, and you will be able to identify and release negative past-oriented thoughts soon after they come up.

Release the Future

Releasing the future may be a bit trickier for some people. If you are frustrated with your current job, house, relationship status, financial situation, or relationship with yourself, it's difficult to understand how you can find self-love and acceptance in the present. You may be tempted to cling to the future in the hope that it will bring something better. However, by doing this, you are missing the opportunity to find even the smallest amount of joy, contentment, or connection in the present. You may be neglecting or abandoning your present self. If doing this becomes a habit, you won't know how to fully enjoy the things you wanted when they do eventually show up. Resisting uncomfortable present moments trains you to resist the present in general. This will leave you unable to accept and enjoy the good moments later on.

Releasing the future doesn't mean never making plans, being prepared, or working toward a better situation for yourself. It means releasing how much space the future occupies in your mind. The future is another barrier that prevents us from fully accessing self-love in the present. The promise that you will be worthy of self-love and acceptance "one day" robs you of the realization that you deserve both of these things right now.

Accept the Present

This week's activities will help you notice your thought patterns that remove you from the present and prevent you from accepting yourself as you are. When we settle the mind's tendency to steer away from the current reality, we can fully show up, right here and right now. We can begin to release distracting storylines. We can begin to uncover the ways that you can work toward self-love, no matter how far you are from "where you want to be."

This week's goal is to work toward accepting yourself, accepting your current situation, and accepting that even here, even now, you deserve to treat yourself well. With that notion in mind, let us begin.

Week 1 Daily Affirmations

As this is our first week, choose an affirmation and close your eyes. Ask yourself how you can incorporate this affirmation into your life today. You can use affirmations to help get your mind back on track if it gravitates toward negative thoughts. You can write the affirmation in a journal, write it on a piece of paper and stick it somewhere visible in your home or workspace, meditate on it, or use it in any other way you please.

"I release storylines of the past and future. I show up for myself in the present, over and over again."

"I exhale the past now. As I inhale, I feel profound love and acceptance for myself."

"I release my grip on the future. I am present."

"I am entering a state of unwavering self-acceptance."

"Each moment is a new opportunity to treat myself lovingly."

"I deserve to receive caring and nurturing treatment from myself."

"I am worthy of self-love, right here and now."

Week 1 Healing Activities

1. **Future Release Meditation:** Sit in a comfortable, upright position. Breathe deeply, in through your nose and out through your mouth. Imagine each of your worries about the future is a string attached to your chest. These strings

expand infinitely out in front of you, tugging on your chest and pulling you forward.

One by one, begin to snip each string with a pair of glowing, golden scissors. With each string you cut loose, you begin to feel lighter and more in control of your body. Stick with the visualization until you have cut away each worry and are free from the tugging of the strings. Notice how your body feels, newly released from the hold of the future.

2. **Action Step, Identify Your Storylines**: Find a journal or create a document you can use for writing prompts in this book. You may enjoy collecting other notes or discoveries you come across through this process.

At the top of the page, write one column labeled "past," and another labeled "future." In these columns, write down any negative, recurring thoughts you have about the past and the future.

Notice which thoughts come up first. Notice which list is longer. Make any notes about how you feel mentally and physically when these thoughts come up. Turn the page in your journal and write about how you plan to shift to the present when these thoughts come up.

3. **Acceptance Self-hypnosis:** Read this script before you begin, making any adjustments you'd like, to create a personal script for your recording. Once you've finished, record yourself saying the script slowly and clearly in an area with no background noise. Pause for at least ten seconds after each line of text, to give yourself time for visualization. Lie down in a comfortable position, relax your body, and replay the recording.

"Breathe in, and breathe out. Follow your breath as your stomach rises and falls.

Each time you breathe in, notice your eyelids getting heavier. Each time you breathe out, notice the muscles around your face relax more and more.

Complete five cycles of breath. On the fifth round, your eyes are closed and your body is deeply relaxed.

Notice the softness of your muscles now that they are relaxed. The relaxation continues to wash over you like a warm bath of water with each deep inhale and full exhale.

Allow yourself to float along in this warm bath. This warmth you feel is the present. In this bath you feel so profoundly safe and secure. You feel the current pull all thoughts of the past or future downstream and away from you. This state of being is so simple. Being present is so easy for you now.

As you sink deeper into relaxation, notice how easily you are accepting yourself and your current situation. Self-acceptance comes to you with ease, and you begin to extend acceptance to everything else in your world. You have found an ease in the present moment. You know you can tap into this feeling of self-acceptance at any moment.

Sinking even deeper into hypnosis, you let the warm water start to carry you now. You are so relaxed. You know you do not need to control the movement, or worry about where you are headed. You float along with ease like this, accepting your situation with the most confidence, and trusting your mind and body to provide you with everything you need in the present.

Offer yourself pure acceptance now. You are doing so well. This is a magnificent and powerful offering of self-love. You know that you can offer yourself this same acceptance and love at any time. You are starting to do this more already, just by being here now.

You come back to awareness now with ease. Start to come back to consciousness by wiggling your fingers and toes. Blink your eyes open and carry this acceptance and love with you as you continue your day."

Week 1 Reflection

1. Take some time to free-write your thoughts on how this week went. What did you enjoy? What was difficult? Which activities would you like to use again in the future?

2. Once you've reflected a bit about the week, come up with your own self-acceptance affirmation that sums up what you've learned. Try to pick a simple affirmation that can help you come back to the present whenever you get stuck on worries of the past or future.

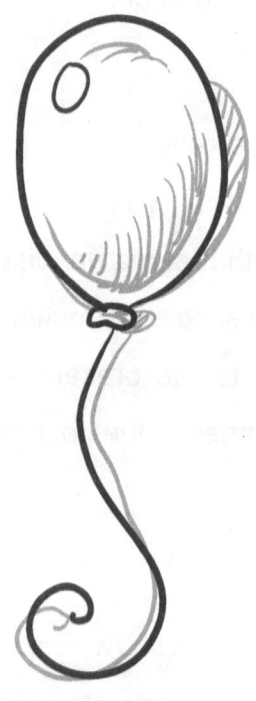

Chapter 2

The First Steps Toward Self-Love

"Go back and take care of yourself. Your body needs you, your perceptions need you, your feelings need you. The wounded child in you needs you. Your suffering needs you to acknowledge it."

Thich Nhat Hanh

(*Reconciliation: Healing the Inner Child*, 2010)[3]

Take a second to think of a time when you've assumed the role of a caretaker. Maybe you have experience taking care of a child or training a puppy? If you were trying to explain a new rule, did the being in your care immediately behave without wiggling or protesting in some way? Chances are, the answer is no. Children love to test authority and choose their own way of doing things. Puppies may want to learn and gain your approval, but their little energetic bodies do not always cooperate. Both operate best when rewarded and praised for their progress. If you've had an experience like this, you know that while it may be frustrating, you are most successful in a caretaking role when you are patient, gentle, and kind. Do you think offering your mind this same care could be a useful approach?

Can you see how treating your mind like a child or small animal in your care may help you become more patient and kind with yourself?

If you consider yourself a good caretaker, are you treating yourself with the same nurturing approach

you offer others?

You know that neglect and harsh criticism don't help anyone progress, learn, and enjoy life. Can you see why these are not useful approaches to your relationship with yourself either?

Now that we've discussed the importance of returning to the present to develop self-love, you may be squirming in your seat a bit. This is normal. Over time, we've all developed one way or another to distract ourselves from thinking about things that cause us discomfort or pain. If your relationship with yourself is one of those uncomfortable things, you may be tempted to use one of your old strategies to flee. You may even be tempted to close this book altogether, but stick with me. This week we're going to ease into things and find a playful yet intentional approach to self-love.

Is This When We Start the Bubble Baths and Manicures?

This is the biggest stereotype about the topic of self-love, so it's worth dissecting a bit here. Self-love has become a cultural phenomenon, encouraging its practitioners to "treat themselves" to a face mask, massage, or luxurious soak in the tub. Yes, all of these things are great, but it's important that these efforts don't become yet another distraction or excuse for avoiding the difficult parts of life.

Cultivating fun self-love routines is worthwhile as long as they are backed up with awareness and intention, and are not simply a means of mental escape. Let's take a look at a few of the "cliché" self-love activities. The chart below demonstrates how the same activity can either be a distraction or a deliberate gesture of kindness, depending on the intention you put behind it.

"Cliché" Self-Love Activity	Distraction/ Self-Critical Mentality	Self-Loving Mentality
A Manicure	"I have been such a mess lately. Getting a manicure will at least give others the impression that I have it all together, and help me avoid my emails for a while."	"I have had a lot on my plate lately. I deserve to take a break to reflect, unwind, and engage in an activity that I know improves my mood."
A Bubble Bath	"I'm such a failure. I can't even take care of myself. At least a bubble bath will make it seem like I am treating myself well."	"I may have had a rough week, but I deserve to reward myself for the small wins I've had anyway."
Going to a Yoga Class	"I have been so lazy lately. The least I can do is make it to one yoga class. Plus, it will help me avoid the laundry piling up at home."	"I've felt off lately. Yoga helps me feel focused and calm, and I deserve to feel that way, no matter how productive I am."
Going on Vacation	My life is so overwhelming. I need to get away from my problems and toxic relationships for a while. Maybe I will never come back!"	"I know that I cannot run from my problems. Despite the inevitable chaos in life, I will allow myself to enjoy a bit of respite and return with a clear mind."

From Punishment to Praise

It can be quite shocking to realize that the same activity could either be self-loving or self-punishing, depending on the intention behind it. A yoga class can be a punishment if you are guilt-tripping yourself into it with thoughts of laziness or shame. It could also be a way of rewarding yourself for getting through a tough week, or an effort in shifting to a more loving inner dialogue. We'll discuss this inner voice more later on, but it's worth reflecting a bit now on the actions you take for yourself throughout the day. Are your actions, and the thoughts behind those actions, a form of punishment, or an act of praise and celebration? Do you go to the gym out of shame for your body, or to celebrate your strength and continue growing? Do you take a vacation to honor your own need for rest or adventure, or as a way to leave your problems behind temporarily?

You may already have a solid foundation for self-love routines in your life. This idea of intention can take them from activities rooted in negativity, insecurity, or fear, and shift them to deeply loving and nurturing habits. Checking in with your thoughts throughout the day can help remind you to steer back to self-love if you get distracted or enter a negative headspace. If you're unsure whether some activity in your life is an act of self-love, a distraction, or a form of self-punishment, ask yourself these questions to gain some clarity:

1. **What is the intention behind this activity?**
2. **Am I operating out of love or fear?**
3. **After engaging in this activity, do I feel better or worse about myself?**
4. **Am I choosing to engage in the activity out of personal preference, or because I believe others want me to?**
5. **Does this activity feel like it is caring for and honoring my inner self, or causing more internal chaos?**

Ask these questions, and come up with some of your own that you can use throughout the day. This can help you make sure that you are operating from a loving headspace. The act of checking in is very repetitive, but the more you develop this skill, the more natural it will begin to feel.

Take Care of Yourself

Going back to this idea that the "outer self" is the caretaker of the "inner self," we can dispel the idea that self-love has to be big gestures of treating ourselves. Instant gratification immediately feels great, but that feeling may be fleeting. Just like caring for a child, self-love isn't always giving gifts and treats. It can sometimes be more mundane, like organizing a shelf, getting your car washed, doing your taxes early, or washing your hair. The difference is, we may dread activities like these in the short term, but we know in the long-term, our future selves will be thankful, and we will begin to repair the relationship with ourselves. When we consistently take action to show up for ourselves, we begin to trust ourselves more. We learn that we can rely on ourselves for the daily care we need, so we begin to feel less mental chaos. Love and care begin to override fear and punishment. We slowly can begin to live better, more joyful lives.

Laugh a Little

Try not to take this process too seriously. A small dose

of humor goes a long way when it comes to developing a self-loving lifestyle. Learn to laugh at your self-punishing, fearful inner self. Coax that self into softening a bit. They have been cruel to you because they are hurting, but they want nothing more than some gentle love and care. Just like a child who is afraid of the monster under their bed, if they choose to laugh at their biggest fear, it begins to shrink and become more manageable.

Find the angle on self-love that feels right for you. This is the first step to finding routines and habits that you will stick with. Find ways of incorporating a playful, light-hearted mindset, so that the most vulnerable parts of yourself feel safe rather than frightened. These fun aspects of self-love are not the whole picture, but they are surely important and worthwhile. So, take that bubble bath, eat that slice of cake, paint your nails green, and laugh at your inner monster. Just remember to stay honest with yourself, keep checking in, and maintain an underlying intention of self-love.

Week 2 Daily Affirmations

As we take the first steps toward intentional self-love, remember to approach the process with a nurturing, caring mindset. Intention, care, celebration, and humor are all great ingredients to consider when forming self-love practices that work well for you. The affirmations for this week incorporate these elements to help you explore an intentional mindset and learn the way your inner self prefers to be treated.

Remember: Self-love is operating out of love, not fear. Self-love is celebration, not punishment or distraction. Self-love is strengthening your actions by putting a firm intention behind them. Self-love is learning to befriend your shadows and laugh when you stumble over them.

"I am my own best caretaker."

"I know, better than anyone, how I prefer to love and be loved."

"I am learning to befriend my inner self."

"The intention behind my self-loving actions is rooted in care and trust."

"I celebrate myself for who I am today."

"I can laugh when I stumble, and remain proud despite my imperfections."

"I am walking into a new chapter of life that is filled with self-love, joy, and confidence."

Week 2 Healing Activities

1. **Inner Love Meditation:** Find a comfortable position to sit with your eyes closed. Take a deep breath in, and exhale slowly and fully. Repeat this until your body feels fully relaxed. Now imagine yourself as a child, getting as specific as possible with the image, what you are wearing, where you are, and any other details that come up. Sit across from your inner child and hold their hands. Tell them you are here to care for them. Continue to sit with them for a few

minutes, coming back to the visual of your inner child sitting across from you each time your mind drifts away.

2. **Action Step**: Think of an activity you liked to do as a child. Maybe you loved playing outside, drawing, or playing a certain sport. Find time this week to incorporate a childhood hobby into your day. Let yourself find some joy in this activity no matter how foreign it feels to you now, simply honoring your inner child with a bit of play. Check in with your body during this activity, making sure to take care of it, note how it feels, and physically relax throughout the process.

3. **Self-Care Hypnosis:** Read this script before you begin, making any adjustments you'd like to create a personal script for your recording. Once you've finished, record yourself saying the script slowly and clearly in an area with no background noise. Pause for at least ten seconds after each

line of text to give yourself time for visualization. Lie down in a comfortable position, relax your body, and replay the recording.

"Breathe in, and breathe out. Allow your breath to be loud and full, making a sound like the waves of the ocean.

Just breathe in now, going to that relaxed place. Each time you breathe out, allow your shoulders to relax and lower a bit more.

Continue listening to your breath as if it were the waves of the ocean. Watch the tide roll in on the inhale, and out on the exhale. Each time the tide rolls in your feel yourself go deeper into a relaxed state.

Notice how effortlessly the tide rolls in and out. You smell the salt air and feel the wind rush along your skin. The sun warms you and you feel simply at peace.

You begin to walk along the shoreline, feeling the soft sand beneath your feet. Your body feels easy and gentle as you stroll along. As you continue to walk, you *begin to see a figure in the distance. This figure looks familiar and innocent.*

You continue walking toward the figure. With each step, you sink deeper into relaxation. The figure becomes more clear, and finally as you approach them, you realize this figure is you.

You are so relaxed, and you approach yourself with a gentle kindness. You embrace yourself and smile. You say to yourself, "You are doing so well. You are doing this exactly right." You continue walking now, side by side with yourself. You are so content as you just walk, listening to the ocean waves.

You are overcome with the belief that you are an innocent creature, worthy of care. You extend care and nurturing to the being walking next to you. You know that you can offer yourself this same care and love at any time. You are starting to do this more. Every time you hear this sound of the ocean breath, you will remember the innocent and worthy being that you are.

You come back to awareness now with ease. Start to come back to consciousness by wiggling your fingers and toes. Blink your eyes open slowly. Carry this feeling of nurturing self-care with you as you stand up and continue with your day."

Week 2 Reflection

1. Take some time to free-write your thoughts on how this week went. What did you enjoy? What was difficult? Which activities would you like to use again in the future?

2. Once you've reflected a bit about the week, come up with your own affirmation that sums up what you've learned about cultivating an intentional, nurturing self-love practice. Try to pick a simple affirmation that can help you find humor, celebration, and confidence in your daily life.

Chapter 3

Embrace the Vulnerability
of Self-Care

"Vulnerability sounds like truth and feels like courage. Truth and courage aren't always comfortable, but they're never weakness."

Brene Brown (*Daring Greatly*, 2012)[4]

Have you ever been the odd one out in an argument? Imagine you are with a group of friends, and the group begins gossiping about a friend that isn't present. It makes you uncomfortable, but you feel self-conscious about speaking up. It's so much easier just to stay quiet, nod, and laugh along with your friends. In your head, you debate whether to stick up for your friend, voice your discomfort, and risk being shamed by the group. In this situation, being accepted socially comes at odds with acting in alignment with your values. This is a common dilemma in life, so use the example scenario as an opportunity to dig deeper.

Is the short-term gratification of social acceptance worth the long-term feeling of disappointment of not sticking up for yourself and your friend?

Do you see how taking risks to honor your values may be the more self-loving option in the long-run?

Do you think acting in alignment with your values, while vulnerable and sometimes scary, would lead

to more self-love in the long-run?

Choosing to stand up for our values will always be a vulnerable endeavor. Building a self-love practice is also a vulnerable endeavor. Both of these acts force us to forgo instant gratification and take a look at what feels true to us. We have to be okay with feeling soft, vulnerable, and open to the judgment of others. We have to be okay with going against the grain, slowing down, admitting we have reached our limits, or admitting we need help. The vulnerability of taking care of ourselves, or even admitting that we need care in the first place, may be why some avoid this topic. However, when we embrace self-care and vulnerability, they make our self-love practices so much richer.

Getting Comfortable with Vulnerability

Self-love is vulnerable because sometimes, the people around you don't actually *want* you to put yourself first. If you're used to prioritizing the desires of others before your own, choosing to honor yourself might disrupt old relationship dynamics. At this stage, you need to be ready for two things to happen:

1. **You need to be ready to be challenged for your decision to choose yourself.**
2. **You need to be ready to stick with the decision, even if it causes a disruption or conflict.**

Though sometimes this can cause disruption, usually, we magnify the impact in our minds. No, choosing yourself doesn't mean deliberately hurting the people around you. It means having the courage to think about what you want, and honor yourself by making the desire known. This can play out in even the simplest of scenarios. Imagine you are making dinner plans with a group of coworkers. The group is trying to decide between burgers, tacos, or sushi. You've been wanting to try the sushi place for months, and don't care for the other two options. It would be so simple to voice this, but you don't want to sway the group, and you know you can find something on any menu. We tend to think people prefer friends that are easygoing, but in this case, most people would actually prefer to know your preference.

This example may seem silly, but even the small decisions in our lives add up. Each time you take the risk of voicing your preference, no matter how simple, you get to know yourself a bit better. You tell yourself that your preferences matter. You take a bit of power back in your life, and your inner self feels the love in these gestures. Here are a few more examples of small gestures that can actually help you practice being vulnerable and voicing your truth:

- Telling your partner you'd like to go on a date this week
- Asking to take a short break to drink some water during a meeting
- Telling your family you need half an hour of alone time in the evenings
- Leaving a party when you are ready to go, even if you're the first one to leave
- Telling your friends that you would prefer not to participate in gossip

- Asking for help with a household chore
- Asking a friend for advice
- Asking to sit outside if the noise in the restaurant is bothering you

As you can see, there are actually quite a few opportunities throughout the day for you to stick up for yourself. Sometimes the small desires we have can feel so meaningless that we don't even give them a second thought. If you feel like you don't even know your own preferences sometimes, tuning into these small moments can help you strengthen that inner knowledge. Getting comfortable with vulnerability will help you get to know and learn to trust yourself. Each time you honor your preferences, you strengthen the message of self-love that you are sending to your inner self.

The Vulnerability of Self-Care

Strengthening your ability to be vulnerable is a key ingredient for consistent self-care. Self-care is taking deliberate action to nurture your inner self. If you have been hard on yourself in the past, it can also be vulnerable for your inner self to acknowledge and accept new gestures of self-love. Just like a child, your inner self may be skeptical of something they haven't yet learned to trust. If you feel resistance to developing a self-love practice, this could be why. You may find that you are afraid to trust yourself. Maybe trying something new led you to criticize yourself harshly in the past. It takes time, patience, and consistency to repair this relationship with yourself, but I think if you've read this far, you know this endeavor is worthwhile.

In order to be vulnerable, we need to feel safe to be our authentic selves. On the path to self-love, this means learning to feel at home in our own skin. Maybe your body and mind have not felt like the safest places to be in the past. Maybe you are hard on yourself. Maybe you endure mental or physical stress to punish yourself for not being good enough. Maybe you suppress certain emotions or try to numb any pain you feel. These are all ways we can teach ourselves that our bodies and minds are not safe places. Once we learn this, we accept it as a fact. It becomes subconscious, and we don't give it much thought. It takes some undoing and relearning to get to a place where we feel safe in our bodies and minds again. Here are a few examples of ways you can begin to feel more comfortable and safe within your body and mind:

Action:	The message that sends to your inner self:
Do some stretches before bed.	I love my body and believe that it deserves to feel relaxed and clam.
Journal some positive thoughts about yourself.	I may not be perfect, but I love myself anyway. I deserve a mind that loves me rather than punishes me.
Take some time to enjoy a nice drink with no screens or distractions.	I deserve to create a calming, restorative space to relax my body and mind.
Plan a morning routine that you are excited to wake up for.	My needs are unique to me. They are worth learning and honoring. I am willing to do what it takes to trust myself again.

For some people, it can be challenging to see the point in forming new habits, putting in a bit of extra effort, and sticking with something you may feel you don't have time for. Trust me, I get it. But these tiny actions are where big change can happen. Learn to see your body and mind as your home. Build the home up with kind thoughts, loving care, and calming routines. Put your preferences at the forefront, and show yourself that this is the new way the house is run. Slowly, you'll begin to feel safe opening up and living fully within your own space.

Making Self-Care Tangible

You may not always relate to the examples I give when discussing vulnerability and self-care, and that's okay. With any program like this, it is important for you to take what feels right, leave what doesn't, and begin learning the skills to map out your own self-love practice. I want you to be able to walk away with your own ideas about what feels right for your body, mind, and inner self. Take the lessons you find here and get as specific as you can with your own relationship with yourself. At the end of the day, it is you who has to live in the home you create in your body and mind. You need to build it to meet your needs and your needs alone. Here are a few ideas for getting specific with your self-care. Take these ideas and morph them into your own personal mind-map for how to add a bit of self-care into your day.

- I will wake up at 7:00 am and drink a glass of water while I meditate.
- I will take five minutes each evening at 9:00 pm to breathe and drink some tea.
- I will take five minutes during my lunch break to stretch my muscles before going back to work.
- I will swap scrolling through social media with ten minutes of reading before bed.
- I will journal each evening to practice creating a positive mental space.
- I will practice listening to my gut reaction instead of dismissing it when asked to make decisions in a group setting.
- I will listen to my nervous system when I become anxious in social settings, and learn to make adjustments to promote physical and mental calm.

These suggestions are just to give you an idea of how you can create tangible self-care habits in your daily life. It is important to go from the idea of loving yourself to taking regular self-loving actions that feel good to you. Feel free to jot some of your ideas down in your journal before moving forward with this week's activities.

Week 3 Daily Affirmations

This week's affirmations are all about the importance of leaning into vulnerability to create a consistent self-love practice. Allow these affirmations to help you as you begin building a nurturing home within your own mind and body.

"In vulnerable moments, I know that I have my own back."

"I take daily steps to show myself the care and love that I deserve."

"I honor my values in each moment of my life."

"I always choose the option that honors my present self and nurtures my future self."

"I am creating a home within my body and mind that feels safe and loving."

"I live a life abundant in caring, nurturing activities."

"My thoughts are becoming more naturally caring and self-loving each day."

Week 3 Healing Activities

1. **Inner Home Meditation:** Find a comfortable position to sit with your eyes closed. Take a deep breath in, and exhale slowly and fully. Repeat this until your body feels fully relaxed. Now imagine you are sitting in a cozy room, the details of the room do not matter, but you feel safe, relaxed, and fully open. Allow yourself to create a home that feels exactly like you want it to. Once you have relaxed into your home,

repeat the phrase in your head: I am safe here. I am safe here. I am safe here. Continue to repeat the phrase and breathe for a few minutes, acknowledging that your body and mind are a loving and nurturing space for you to dwell.

2. **Self-Care Action Step**: Remember that list of specific self-care steps we created at the end of the chapter? If you didn't create one, take time to jot down a few very specific ideas for self-care. This week, try to incorporate just one of these steps into your daily routine. Maybe you stretch for five minutes in the morning, or go on a short walk during your lunch break, or read for ten minutes in the evening. Try to stick with it, taking it just one day at a time. Notice how you feel after a week of this new habit.

3. **Self-hypnosis:** Read this script before you begin, making any adjustments you'd like to create a personal script for your recording. Once you've finished, record yourself saying the script slowly and clearly in an area with no background

noise. Pause for at least ten seconds after each line of text to give yourself time for visualization. Lie down in a comfortable position, relax your body, and replay the recording.

"Begin to breathe in, slowly observing as your lungs fill with fresh air. Breathe out and release any muscle tension you notice in your body.

Place your hands on your belly in a way that feels natural. They create a space where your belly can rise and fall with ease. This comforting gesture helps you sink even deeper into relaxation.

Just enter that inner space now, going to that inner home that opens up with such ease. You feel as safe and secure as your stomach does, rising and falling beneath your hands.

Each time you breathe in, you notice your inner world expanding. Each time you exhale, you relax even deeper, surrendering to the safety you feel in your own beautiful space.

A flickering flame appears in front of you. It dances as you breathe, and warms you from within. You are overcome with the knowledge that no matter how deeply you breathe, no matter how uncertain you feel, this flame will not be extinguished.

You feel this flame warming your belly, kept safe by your protective hands. You are so relaxed by this safety and warmth. You are beginning to trust this space more and more.

You realize that the safety you feel here, the warmth, and the beautiful light, are growing stronger the longer you dwell in this space. The more time you spend in this loving home, the more you accept it and allow it to protect you.

You know now that honoring your values and staying true to yourself are all about this sense of home. You know this space is always here for you. You know it will protect you, so there is no need to feel unsure. You accept this space and trust it completely now.

Carry the warmth you feel all the way back to a sense of awareness. Start to come back to consciousness by wiggling your fingers and toes. Open your eyes, and carry on with your day, knowing you carry home with you wherever you go."

Week 3 Reflection

1. Take some time to free-write your thoughts on how this week went. What did you enjoy? What was difficult? Which activities would you like to use again in the future?

2. Once you've reflected a bit about the week, come up with your own self-care affirmation that sums up what you've learned about the value of being vulnerable. Try to pick a simple affirmation that can remind you of the importance of staying true to your values.

Chapter 4

Dive Deep to Learn Your Authentic Truth

"Only the truth of who you are, if realized, will set you free."

Eckhart Tolle (*A New Earth*, 2005)[5]

Think back to a time when anger or sadness overcame you. Maybe you find that these emotions frequently overwhelm you and cause you pain. Perhaps one time you got so angry that you shouted at someone you loved, slammed a door, stormed out, or made another rash decision that you regretted later. We often allow the pain of emotions like anger and sadness to make our decisions for us. We become so uncomfortable that we lash out, run away, or become paralyzed and unable to address the problem. This happens to all of us at some point, but usually, the aftermath leaves us feeling regretful. Maybe we hurt a loved one, or maybe we even hurt ourselves. Avoiding pain only causes us more pain, so what if we could train ourselves to approach these situations differently?

Do you notice any tendencies in yourself when dealing with emotions like anger and sadness?

Diving into these tendencies may be scary, but do you think it would be worth it if it meant you could stop repeating them?

Is the discomfort of sitting with yourself during stressful situations or overwhelming emotions worth enduring for the sake of self-love?

This topic may lead to more resistance than you have felt in previous chapters, and that's okay. Just remember that developing negative tendencies is normal. We do this to minimize the pain we feel in certain situations. It is just a side-effect of being human. However, sometimes we need to check-in with our tendencies to see whether they are helping us or hurting us. We may have outgrown behaviors that were once helpful for us somehow. Be patient with yourself this week; it has the potential to provide a bit of relief and deepen your self-love practice profoundly.

Dig into Your Emotional Tendencies

A big part of self-love is rediscovering the positive aspects of yourself that you may have stopped seeing. However, once you develop a less critical, more curious and loving relationship with yourself, it is important not to bypass the elements that may be holding you back. If we gravitate toward the positive and overlook the negative completely, we miss out on significant and crucial opportunities for growth. We also deny ourselves the opportunity to accept ourselves fully. It's time to trust yourself to examine negative tendencies without judgment. This, in itself, is an act of self-love.

Let's explore some examples of negative tendencies to help you pinpoint what yours may be:

"Negative" Emotion	Behavior in Response to the Emotion
Anger	Anger Lashing out, shouting at people, running away from the situation, saying things you don't mean, throwing things or slamming doors, becoming unable to see a middle ground
Sadness	Numbing the emotion with unhealthy eating or drinking habits, suppressing the feeling, acting out angry behaviors instead of addressing sadness, putting up walls, surrounding yourself with people or activities to distract you from feeling sad
Guilt	Harshly critiquing yourself, shaming yourself relentlessly, replaying scenarios in your head, hiding from certain people or situations
Jealously	Comparing yourself to others, thinking negative thoughts about yourself, withdrawing socially, putting down other people, engaging in gossip
Self-doubt	Putting yourself down, critiquing yourself mentally and physically, isolating yourself, judging or putting down other people, withdrawing socially, pretending to be someone you are not, acting out of alignment with your values

I've put the word "negative" in quotations intentionally here. Sure, some emotions are more painful than others, but all emotions are important, and we don't get out of experiencing any of them. The way we behave when we feel certain emotions provides us with useful information if we allow ourselves to see it. If you can be patient and view how you respond to certain emotions, you can learn key information for moving forward and taking better care of yourself.

Be Patient with Difficult Emotions

The fun and easy sides of self-love are understandably more pleasant to engage with. However, sifting through the more difficult feelings and emotions is just as, if not more important. If you've made it this far, you have shown yourself that self-love is a worthy endeavor. Don't stop now. The more unpleasant emotions may feel good to avoid in the short-term, but addressing the way we process them can help us get to a much healthier, happier, and more self-loving place.

The key ingredient for working through this phase of the process is patience. If you can be patient with yourself, the abilities to change and grow a solid self-love practice are well within reach. Take some time to write out some of your tendencies and how you want to work on changing them. If you are satisfied with the way you respond to a certain emotion, write out why. Here are some examples of how this may look:

- **When I am angry**, I often shout at my partner and say hurtful things I regret later. **I want to work toward responding to anger by** taking a break to leave, breathe, and come back to address the problem with a clearer mind and calmer body.
- **When I am sad**, I often try to drown out the emotion by burying myself in work and socializing. **I want to work toward responding to sadness by** giving myself time and space to slow down, cry if I need to, and fully process the emotion before diving back into work.
- **When I feel self-doubt**, I often withdraw from social settings and isolate myself. **I want to**

work toward responding to self-doubt by taking a break to gather my thoughts, remind myself that I am worthy and loved, and spend time with people who help me feel seen and heard.

No matter what your tendencies are, do not shame yourself or get frustrated. You are the way you are for a reason, and now you can take back some control and steer yourself toward behaviors that you would prefer to have. A bit of patience and effort will go a long way, and you will eventually be glad you took the time to sit with your difficult emotions and tendencies.

Honor Your Authentic Self

Honoring your authentic self is more than just examining difficult emotions. Your responses to positive emotions are worth exploring, as well. Do you allow yourself to feel happiness completely? Do you cover up feelings of excitement or love because you don't want to appear silly or weak? Showing up as your true self when feeling positive emotions can feel vulnerable as well. Maybe we don't want to show people the things that make us happy, because we are afraid they will get taken away. Maybe we don't want to express love, because we are afraid we will be rejected. Take some time to explore your positive emotions in your journal as well. Here are some examples of how this may look:

- **When I am happy**, I often minimize my own joy by focusing on my shortcomings. **I want to work toward responding to happiness by** allowing myself to feel happy, and tell others that I am happy without judging myself.
- **When I feel love**, I often suppress the feeling or change the subject altogether. **I want to work toward responding to feelings of love by** expressing it outwardly through loving words and actions.
- **When I feel hope**, I often talk myself out of it by thinking negative thoughts. **I want to work toward responding to hope by** writing down the thought that made me feel hopeful and putting energy toward thinking similar positive

thoughts.

No matter how uncomfortable you feel exploring the behaviors you want to change, I hope you realize that the discomfort is not permanent. Diving deep, sitting with the discomfort, and being patient with yourself will lead toward meaningful change in time. When you take this time to get to know yourself better and guide yourself toward healthier behaviors, you show yourself the self-love you have been longing for.

Week 4 Daily Affirmations

The affirmations for this week encourage you to be patient, focus on self-discovery, and know that you can release negative behaviors. Even if you have always thought your personality was fixed, you can always change, and self-love will help you get there. Be gentle with yourself, allow it to take the necessary amount of time, and open up to your authentic self.

"I am patient with myself through difficult emotions."

"I honor my truth in all areas of life."

"My path to self-discovery is fruitful, joyful, and never-ending."

"My authenticity shines because I love myself well."

"I learn from my negative behaviors and release them readily."

"I know myself intimately and love myself fully."

"I release anything I have been carrying that is not in alignment with my truth."

Week 4 Healing Activities

1. **Authentic Self Meditation:** Find a comfortable position to sit with your eyes closed. Take a deep breath in, and exhale slowly and fully. Repeat this until your body feels fully relaxed. Imagine you are sitting beneath many colorful layers of

fabric. These fabrics feel heavy and weigh you down. One by one, a force begins pulling the fabrics away. With each fabric removed, you feel lighter, you can breathe more fully, and your inner light can shine brighter. Continue the meditation until the last fabric is pulled away, revealing your inner light and allowing you to feel so light that you begin floating. Your authentic self is present, as it always was, and is now free to shine its brightest.

2. **Emotions journaling action step**: Pick one difficult emotion (e.g., sadness, anger, jealousy) and one emotion you enjoy (e.g., happiness, love, gratitude). Each day, keep a list of times these emotions came up, and how you responded to them. At the end of the week, see if any patterns emerge regarding your behaviors. Does observing these behaviors help you feel like you could change them? Did noticing any joyful moments allow you to enjoy them more fully?

3. **Authenticity Self-hypnosis:** Read this script before you begin, making any adjustments you'd like, to create a personal script for your recording. Once you've finished, record yourself saying the script slowly and clearly in an area with no background noise. Pause for at least ten seconds after each line of text to give yourself time for visualization. Lie down in a comfortable position, relax your body, and replay the recording.

"Close your eyes and breathe easily, in through your nose and out through your mouth.

Place your hands on your heart, feeling the warmth and allowing it to radiate through your chest.

The warmth in your chest is starting to become bright and vibrant. Your chest is glowing bright green, like a beautiful, lush forest. You feel your chest rise and fall as you sink deeper into relaxation.

Each time you breathe in, you notice the light in your chest growing brighter. Each time you exhale, you relax even deeper, and watch as the light catches difficult emotions, allowing them to glow bright too.

This bright green light is transmuting everything into a warm and glowing positive force within you. You know you are so much more than your behaviors. You know this glowing light is uncovering your authentic truth.

The light is melting away all the walls and masks you've held up for so long. You are so relaxed by the knowledge that you are free from these things. You are allowing your authentic truth to show itself. This is an effortless, joyful, vibrant feeling.

You can see that this light, your authenticity, has the power to heal your body and mind. As you let this light completely relax your body, you notice it also smoothing out and relaxing your mind.

You see that there was never anything between you and your authentic self. You easily see your authentic truth. You know you can operate as this most authentic, confident, and truly happy version of yourself at all *times.*

Allow this beautiful green light to linger as you tap back into awareness. Start to come back to consciousness by wiggling your fingers and toes. Open your eyes and take a deep breath, knowing the most authentic version of you is still here with you now."

Week 4 Reflection

1. Take some time to free-write your thoughts on how this week went. What did you enjoy? What was difficult? Which activities would you like to use again in the future?

2. Once you've reflected a bit about the week, come up with your own self-discovery affirmation that sums up what you've learned about digging deep and uncovering the truth within yourself. Try to pick a simple affirmation that can help you stay patient when dealing with difficult emotions.

Chapter 5

Cultivate Undeniable Self-Trust

*"You do not have to be good.
You do not have to walk on your knees
for a hundred miles through the
desert, repenting. You only have to let the
soft animal of your body love what it loves."*

Mary Oliver (*Wild Geese*, 2004)[6]

Imagine it is the start of a new year, and it's time to pick a New Year's resolution. Maybe you try to start a new habit of working out twice a week. You start out strong, going twice a week for a few weeks in January. However, by the time February rolls around, you have to go to the mechanic, or come down with a cold, so you miss a week. After missing that week, you start letting smaller things be excuse enough to miss your workouts. It's too cold outside, or you're tired, or you have too many other chores to tackle. While it's healthy not to be too harsh on yourself about falling short here and there, what do you think this habit is doing for your relationship with yourself?

When you set goals that are unrealistic or unaligned with your values, do you trust yourself to follow through?

When you don't follow through with a goal you've made for yourself, do you think this impacts how much you trust yourself in other areas of life?

Instead of creating big, unsustainable goals, do you

think one small, consistent goal could be enough to help you build trust in yourself again?

This week is all about trusting yourself, why it's challenging, and how to build self-trust in small, loving, and intentional ways. If you are unsure about your level of self-trust, know this. You have made it to chapter 5 of this book. No matter how long it took you to get here, you trusted yourself to work through each chapter in order to build self-love, and now here you are. Allow this to be a moment of celebration, a moment to acknowledge that you must already possess some level of self-trust. Now let's dig in to discover more, and see how we can build upon this feeling.

Feel Confident in Belonging to Yourself

You could say self-trust is the act of belonging to yourself. When we are children, we may feel as though we belong to our parents. We consult them when we have problems, they help us with homework, and they plan out daily schedules for us. So in adulthood, it's important to learn to offer yourself the same support.

You may use the parent-child example as a guideline, or you may be starting from scratch. Either way, learning to belong to yourself is a shift out of self-doubt, and into self-trust. Let's take a look at a few examples of a self-doubting mindset, and how it compares to a more self-trusting approach.

Self-Doubting Mindset	Self-Trusting Mindset
I have a big decision to make, and I am unsure what to do. I will ask everyone I know what they think and make my decision based on their feedback.	I may consult a few important people in my life when making a big decision. However, I know how to reflect internally, listen to my preferences, and trust that I know what is best for myself.
When someone makes a comment that doesn't sit right with me, I keep quiet, knowing I am probably the only one that feels that way.	When something doesn't sit right with me, I stand up for myself, feeling confident that I made the right choice and honored my values well.
I set goals that I have seen other people set. If they can keep them, why shouldn't I be able to?	I check-in with my preferences, needs, and abilities, and set goals that I see as achievable for me personally.
I use excuses to justify falling short in life, but secretly I shame myself for not being good enough.	I know sometimes I will fall short because I am human. I do not shame myself for this, but instead, use it as an opportunity to check-in and reassess my expectations.
My thoughts about myself are usually negative and critical.	My thoughts about myself may be critical at times, but I know how to catch that when it happens and steer toward a more accepting and loving approach.

When you belong to yourself, it doesn't mean you are one hundred percent self-reliant and never need to consult anyone else for anything. It means you know how to trust your intuition, acknowledge your needs and emotions without shaming. It means that you will catch yourself, and accept yourself, when you stumble in life.

When everything you do has an underlying air of self-doubt, you may start to doubt whether you even belong in your own skin. You may operate in self-doubt unknowingly. Self-doubt is a practice that develops over time, through little actions of neglecting your own needs. Self-trust is also a practice that you can develop through little steps of learning to listen to yourself again.

Feeling like you truly belong somewhere is one of the greatest feelings we experience as humans. So, why wouldn't we hope to experience this within our own skin? What would it feel like to belong to yourself? What would it feel like to shift from self-doubt to undeniable trust that you have your own back? Believe it or not, you are capable of achieving this. Here are a few tangible ways you can work to build this feeling within yourself:

- **When making a big decision**, journal about your feelings toward the situation, and your preferred outcome.
- **When you feel uncomfortable socially**, stand up for yourself, or take a bathroom break to breathe and sort out your thoughts.
- **When you set a new goal**, focus on what feels doable and exciting for you personally.
- **When you fall short**, acknowledge your humanity. Practice forgiving yourself. Come up with a plan for how you can better support yourself and make sure you follow through next time.
- **When feeling a big emotion**, allow yourself to feel it fully. Journal, go for a walk with a friend, or find a way to process in the way that feels best for you.
- **When you notice negative thoughts,** work on steering back to an accepting and loving mindset. This does not mean forcing positivity. It simply means creating a supportive inner voice that feels accepting and trustworthy.

Through small gestures, you can slowly build self-trust. Explore which steps feel best for you and how you can begin implementing them into your life.

Acknowledge Your Strengths

Another great way to work on self-trust is by acknowledging your strengths. In which areas of life do you already trust yourself? Maybe you are great at your job and always deliver projects on time. Maybe you are a very loving and forgiving parent or friend. You could be a great driver, chef, gardener, partner, painter, cleaner, reader, or thinker. Take a second to think about the things you know you do well, no matter how big or small. Acknowledge that this is self-trust.

You are willing to admit that your strengths are your strengths because you trust yourself to do these things well. As humans, none of us do *everything* well, but we can always grow and develop new strengths. When we try new things, we don't know whether or not we will perform well. This uncertainty can fuel self-doubt if we let it. But what if you could somehow take the same trust you feel when performing your strengths, and apply it to areas of uncertainty?

Instead of trusting that you will succeed in every area of life, try trusting that you will *do your best*. And if your best does not meet your expectations, you can trust yourself to accept the humanity in that. Trust yourself to try again. Trust that each time, your best will get just a little bit better. This attitude will help you when setting goals. Instead of getting frustrated when you fall short, shaming yourself, thinking negative thoughts, and throwing in the towel, you can take a gentler approach. The approach of trying your best, acknowledging your humanity, and trying again tomorrow can be your new strength with a bit of practice.

Be Realistic and Follow Through

Through these efforts of exploring and practicing self-trust, it's important to be realistic with yourself. Don't set a goal of going to the gym five nights a week if you know you are busy six nights a week. You may be able to start small, build consistency, and eventually establish a routine of five workouts a week. That would be great! But the trick is to develop awareness surrounding your own needs, and develop realistic goals that reflect those needs. This shows your inner self they can trust you to set up a path for success.

Once you've established realistic goals, it's time to follow through. Following through is one of the important ways to develop self-trust. If your goal is to run twice a week, following through sends a message to your inner self that you are trustworthy. Every time you follow through, you strengthen this message, and the self-trust grows deeper. Of course, following through on goals, promises, or habits may not always be possible. Here is a simple guide for how to address these situations to maintain self-trust.

1. **Set a realistic goal.**
2. **Follow through.**
3. **Acknowledge slip-ups and adjust accordingly.**
4. **Establish a check-in, maybe weekly or monthly, to establish whether or not the goal**

is helping build self-trust.
5. **Repeat the tasks of following through and checking in repeatedly.**

Your path to cultivating self-trust will be unique to you, just like every other element of this process. Sit with what you have learned and take time to adjust it for your own needs. Taking what is helpful and tailoring it to align with your preferences is another step toward deepening your level of self-trust.

Week 5 Daily Affirmations

This week's affirmations focus on the concept of belonging to yourself, and learning to trust your decisions, intuition, and preferences. Use them as you explore self-trust in your daily activities. No matter your level of self-trust coming into this week, it's great to take a moment to acknowledge how you feel about this topic, and discover ways to strengthen the trust over time.

"I belong, fully and readily, to myself."

"I trust myself to set goals that are achievable for me."

"I keep the goals I set for myself."

"I trust myself completely, in every aspect of my life."

"I am getting to know myself, learning my strengths, and acknowledging my humanity."

"My self-trust is undeniable, and comes from a deep and honest place within."

"I am the one who makes the best decisions for me."

Week 5 Healing Activities

1. **Meditation:** Sit in a comfortable, upright position on the floor or in a chair. Lower your shoulders and release any tension in the face, jaw, and neck. Begin to breathe fully. When you exhale,

think the words, "I exhale self-doubt." When you inhale, think the words "I trust myself." Practice this deep breathing practice for two or three minutes, continuing to release doubts you feel about yourself on the exhale, and inhale trust and confidence. If you'd like, you can set a timer so that your full focus is on your breathing.

2. **Action Step**: Try to spend one day observing yourself and your levels of self-doubt. Jot down a short note each time you notice self-doubt arise. At the end of the day, observe your notes. Are there any patterns? Were you more doubtful of yourself around certain people, or in certain situations? Make a list of ways you can support yourself in these moments and try to implement them in the days to come.

3. **Self-hypnosis:** Read this script before you begin, making any adjustments you'd like to create a personal script for your recording. Once you've finished, record yourself saying the script slowly and clearly in an area with no background

noise. Pause for at least ten seconds after each line of text to give yourself time for visualization. Lie down in a comfortable position, relax your body, and replay the recording.

"Breathe in through your nose, and out through your mouth, quietly observing as your muscles slowly begin to relax.

Each time you exhale, your muscles relax further into the surface beneath you. You trust the surface to hold you and you relax completely. As your muscles relax more and more, your eyelids naturally grow heavy and begin to close.

You are now at the base of a mountain. You see the gorgeous, towering mountain stretch up above you. You see several paths before you. You select your preferred path and you take your first steps with ease and confidence.

You breathe in the mountain air as you make your way up the path. Each time you come across a forking path, you trust yourself to make the right decision and continue walking with endless confidence.

This ability to trust yourself gets easier and easier the higher up you get on the mountain. You know you are leading yourself in the exact direction you are supposed to go. You continue to breathe in self-trust, and breathe out confidence. You are fully relaxed and content with each step you take.

Now you are getting closer to the top of the mountain. You are flooded with a happy energy. You know that trusting yourself was the right decision. You reach a clearing, and the view at the top of the mountain is unbelievable.

You can see that your ability to make the right decisions for yourself led you here. This stunning view and this feeling of accomplishment show that trusting yourself was the best move. You see that trusting yourself is the easiest, most comforting thing you can do. You are growing more and more relaxed and comfortable with trusting your intuition.

You see that self trust is a beautiful, effortless thing. You can take time to assess, and make the decision to trust yourself with pure confidence.

Trust yourself now as you come back to awareness. Start to come back to consciousness by wiggling your fingers and toes. Open your eyes and carry the feeling you felt at the top of the mountain, the feeling of trust and joy, with you throughout your day."

Week 5 Reflection

1. Take some time to free-write your thoughts on how this week went. What did you enjoy? What was difficult? Which activities would you like to use again in the future?

2. Once you've reflected a bit about the week, come up with your own self-trust affirmation that sums up what you've learned. Try to pick a simple affirmation that can help you move past self-doubt and learn to trust your intuition.

Chapter 6

Protect Your Energy to Find Balance Between Rest and Activity

"Every person needs to take one day away. A day in which one consciously separates the past from the future. Jobs, family, employers, and friends can exist one day without any one of us, and if our egos permit us to confess, they could exist eternally in our absence. Each person deserves a day away in which no problems are confronted, no solutions searched for. Each of us needs to withdraw from the cares which will not withdraw from us."

Maya Angelou

(Wouldn't Take Nothing for My Journey Now, 1993)[7]

In today's fast-paced world, it's not hard to recall a time when you have denied yourself rest. Maybe there was a week where it felt like your to-do list was endless. You felt your eyes getting dry and heavy, your body slowing down, and your mind desperately trying to switch off. Maybe you have even had entire months or years that felt this way. In this situation, it's easy to think that resting would mean neglecting your responsibilities. However, you could also argue that *not* resting means neglecting your own needs.

When your body is tired, do you often push past the urge to rest in order to be more productive?

If you do allow yourself to rest, is that choice often paired with shame or guilt?

When you ignore your mental and physical needs, do you notice any patterns of fatigue, burn out, sickness, isolation, procrastination, or dread?

Life is stressful, and there are certainly moments when slowing down is not possible. I'm not saying drop everything and sleep for four months, although I am sure some of us could use that. I'm simply asking you to get curious. How often do you take stock of your mental and physical state? How often do you allow yourself to rest, completely free of guilt? How often do you shape your daily activities to be nurturing and informed by what is realistic for you? This week, let's consider the roles of rest and activity, and the importance of striking a balance between them. These building blocks are crucial to any self-love practice, so let's dive in and discover which self-loving steps are right for you.

Self-Neglect in Action

Do any bells go off for you when you hear the term self-neglect? Many people today neglect themselves by overworking and not checking in with their bodies and minds. This will eventually lead to burn out. Conversely, too much rest can also be a way of neglecting yourself. Maybe you have a big project due, and it becomes too overwhelming. You isolate yourself, stop spending time with friends, and stop doing the things you know you love because you don't feel you have "earned" them. When we neglect ourselves, we stop asking what our bodies need. We stop asking what our inner selves need. It is not a sustainable way to live, and eventually, our bodies will call this to our attention in one way or another.

Neglecting our needs makes us sick from the inside out. We procrastinate, we shame ourselves, and we repeat. Or we overwork, we get sick, and we repeat. These toxic behaviors corrode our self-worth because they are fueled by guilt. We are teaching our inner selves that they deserve to be punished either mentally or physically. So, how do we remove the guilt when it creeps into our behaviors like this? Here are a few ideas for restoring the balance between rest and activity in your life.

Behavior shift for self-loving rest:	Why it helps:	Example:
Practice compassion	If a child told you they were tired, you wouldn't force them to keep playing. If a friend said they needed to rest, you'd offer understanding and support. You deserve to treat yourself with that same compassion.	Your eyes get heavy after a long day of work. Instead of getting angry at your unfinished tasks, turn off your computer and say, "I did enough today. I am proud of my efforts. I grant myself permission to unwind."
Follow your intuition	Forcing more productivity when you're tired or checking out when you're overwhelmed both shut off your connection to your intuition. Start listening to your gut when you need rest, so you can restore and bounce back faster.	You are at work but find your mind constantly wandering from your current task. Instead of getting frustrated but continuing to procrastinate, try taking an intentional ten-minute break. Let your mind settle before returning to the task.

Build in breaks	Endless streaks of productivity are not natural for the human brain. We need a mix of action and rest, and a healthy variety in our daily activities. Building in breaks will help you see rest as a crucial part of your daily routine instead of something to be ashamed of.	Write one or two ten-minute breaks into your day whenever possible. You can set an alarm or write them into your calendar. Make a point to move your body and get a change of scenery during this time. Consider these plans just as important as your other daily tasks.
Rest IS the activity	Instead of "resting" while talking on the phone, writing an email, or doing another work task, see rest as the activity. Cutting out the urge to multitask will ensure you get full enjoyment out of your restful efforts.	When you rest, avoid using a phone, computer, or any other device that puts your mind elsewhere. Try to use the time to check in with your mind and body and acknowledge that you deserve this time to restore.

As simple as it sounds, the key to this process is remembering that you are human. You are not a machine. You are only capable of so much, and no amount of guilt will magically bring you an endless supply of time and energy. So why not offer yourself a bit of kindness instead? Why not work to transform your relationship with rest? After all, mending this relationship has the potential to transform the rest of your life.

Rest to Transform

What I'm getting at here is the fact that we put a lot of energy into resisting rest, shaming ourselves for needing rest, and mentally checking out rather than giving in to rest. But maybe, just maybe, removing this resistance and mental chatter will prove more helpful. Reclaiming your relationship to rest has the potential to drastically improve your life. Here are a few areas this effort will help transform:

- **Your ability to set and keep boundaries**

- **The quality of your time spent in reflection**
- **Your decision-making skills**
- **Your levels of self-acceptance and self-worth**
- **Your ability to trust yourself**
- **Your ability to heal pain that you have stored in your body**
- **The quality of your inner dialogue**
- **Your productivity**
- **Your level of efficiency**
- **The amount of joy you get out of both rest and activity**

Learning to enjoy rest and make time for it helps mend your relationship with your inner self. You tell that version of you that you are worth more than your level of productivity. Each time you send this message, you strengthen the impact it has. Any good leader knows that showing kindness and understanding will boost the productivity of their team. When people feel heard, and when their needs feel honored, they show up more fully in their roles. They get more done and feel more satisfied at the end of the day. Do you think you could be your own leader in this area? Could you try putting your wellbeing first, just to see what happens?

Finding Ease in Your Activities

We've established that removing shame will establish a more self-loving approach to rest. So, what if we apply the same idea to our activities in life? Many of us take on too much in our roles at work. We push ourselves to accomplish more, faster. Sometimes we even do this with our weekends and free time. We pack all of our downtime with activities to try and make the most of each moment. However, even the activities we enjoy the most, if done in an effort to pressure ourselves, become just another means of self-punishment.

Think about it. Have you ever had a few days off work, and just wanted to spend them resting, watching movies, and maybe going on a few long walks? Maybe the pressure of needing to make the most of the time got the best of you, and you booked a trip to a nearby town. You packed the days full of activities and returned to work feeling just as exhausted as ever. Now, maybe an action-packed trip is your idea of relaxation. Everyone is different. The question is, when you have free time, what is the guiding force in how you decide to spend that time? Is it a gentle, kind, curious approach to meeting your own needs? Is it a mix of guilt, anxiety, and fear of missing out? Is this guiding force similar to the one that guides your efforts at work, and your decisions to rest?

Self-love is all about getting to the root of these questions and starting to work in alignment with your own needs. If you need rest, carve out time for a nice bubble bath or cozy movie on the sofa. If you need some activity to disconnect, plan a hike or a day-trip with friends. Even just taking five minutes to breathe and release muscle tension during your workday can be a big step. Get curious about your needs. Let what you discover steer you toward a few self-loving steps today. Repeat tomorrow.

Week 6 Daily Affirmations

This week's affirmations focus on healing your

relationship with rest. You're encouraged to check in with your mental and physical needs and make compassionate decisions for yourself. Use these affirmations if you feel any resistance toward resting. Get curious about this aspect of your mental dialogue, and be patient as you steer toward a more self-loving approach to thinking about rest.

"I did enough today. I am proud of my efforts. I grant myself permission to unwind."

"I allow myself to rest fully, completely free of worries."

"I choose daily activities based on my personal preferences and needs."

"I operate in communion with my inner self. I am my own best guiding force."

"I notice resistance to rest and let it pass. I choose to care for myself now."

"I am healing my mindset regarding work and rest. I work hard and feel proud. I rest hard and feel proud."

"I vow to check in with my mental and physical needs and honor them. I am building this practice from a place of deep self-respect."

Week 6 Healing Activities

1. **Check-in meditation:** Lay down on a comfortable, flat surface, and close your eyes. Begin to breathe fully in through your nose, and out through your mouth. First, allow your focus to come to your feet. Notice your toes, arches, and ankles. Thank your feet for everything they do for you, and allow them to relax completely. Repeat this process of noticing, thanking, and releasing with your calves, then knees, then thighs. As you work your way up your body, continue checking in and allowing your body to relax more and more. Once you reach the top of your head, allow a feeling of peace to come over

you. Sit in this feeling as long as you like, knowing both your body and mind deserve to relax this deeply.

2. **Action Step**: Take a moment during or after your workday to give yourself a hand massage. Remove any jewelry, use a lotion or oil if that feels nice, and gently massage your hands. Start with the palms and work your way up to the soft skin between each finger. Breathe in and out and let the other muscle tension in your body begin to melt away. Massage all the way to the end of each finger, one at a time. Use this as an opportunity to notice the work your hands do for you each day, how they feel, and how they deserve this moment of rest.

3. **Restful Self-hypnosis:** Read this script before you begin, making any adjustments you'd like to create a personal script for your recording. Once you've finished, record yourself saying the script slowly and clearly in an area with no background noise. Pause for at least ten seconds after each

line of text to give yourself time for visualization. Lie down in a comfortable position, relax your body, and replay the recording.

"Breathe in through your nose and out through your mouth, allowing your face to relax. Continue breathing as you observe your neck muscles and shoulders softening into a restful state.

As you breathe in, you imagine a profound heaviness drifting over your body. When you breathe out, you surrender completely to a restful bliss.

You are surrounded by the most comforting blankets and pillows. You feel warm, safe, and completely relaxed. You know you deserve rest, and you receive it with ease now.

Your breath grows slower and slower. You are surrounded by infinite comforts. You accept the warmth and security you feel as you drift down deeper into a more restful state.

You recognize that letting go and allowing rest to take over is so restorative, here in this deep, relaxed state. You know you are free to access this deep rest at any moment you choose.

You are still drifting down into the sea of cozy blankets and pillows. You feel complete bliss. You know that rest will take over if you just let go. You are learning to let go and trust that you deserve this serene and blissful relaxation. Everything else falls away and you fall into an effortless restful state.

You know that you can and should achieve this deep state of rest every day. This comfortable, infinite, blissful state is yours whenever you want it.

You are building a beautiful balance between activity and rest. You can call upon this restful state with ease. Every night, you fall into this luxurious comfort, and you wake up completely restored.

Start to come back to consciousness by wiggling your fingers and toes. Gently open your eyes and maintain this restful quality in your body and mind. Continue to bring this feeling with you into your other restful activities."

Week 6 Reflection

1. Take some time to free-write your thoughts on how this week went. What did you enjoy? What was difficult? Which activities would you like to use again in the future?

2. Once you've reflected a bit about the week, come up with your own affirmation that sums up what you've learned about the importance of rest. Try to pick a simple affirmation that can help you ease any resistance you feel toward resting your body and mind.

Chapter 7

Create an Inner Voice of Kindness and Compassion

"Remember, you have been criticizing yourself for years and it hasn't worked. Try approving of yourself and see what happens."

Louise Hay (*You Can Heal Your Life*, 1984)[8]

Last week, we discussed the importance of adjusting your inner dialogue surrounding rest. Now, let's take that concept a bit further. What would it be like to have an inner voice that offered kindness before criticism, compassion before shame?

Say you want to ask for a raise at work. You've spent years going above and beyond, and seen many coworkers get raises since you started your job. You've thought of every variable, spoken with your peers, and logically you know you have every right to ask for an increase in salary. But, there is a voice in your head telling you that you're an imposter. The voice says you don't really deserve the raise, or maybe you don't even deserve the job at all. Despite the heaps of evidence that this voice is incorrect, it has still kept you from mustering the courage to ask for the raise.

Do you let the voice in your head convince you to settle for less than you deserve?

Do you find that your thoughts tend to be critical or doubtful rather than encouraging or kind?

Do you get caught up believing your negative thoughts to be true? Do you think this could be holding you back in more than one area of your life?

Many of us tend to have naturally negative inner dialogues. We are critical when we look in the mirror, make mistakes at work, or say the wrong thing in front of friends. We doubt our worth in relationships, and if we receive negative treatment, we may come up with reasons that we deserved to be treated poorly. When we experience the inevitable negativity of life, we feel discomfort or pain, and we are often our own easiest target to blame for the discomfort we feel. However, beating ourselves up through negative self-talk only exacerbates this pain.

Of course, pain is an inevitable part of life, which can be infuriating to accept. However, if this is the case, why are we so willing to increase the pain with a critical inner voice? Wouldn't it be a relief to turn inward and find kindness there instead? Wouldn't creating a compassionate inner voice be the ultimate act of self-love?

Make Peace With Your Inner Voice

Let's take a minute here to remember that we are not looking to critique our current selves. Our inner voices likely do enough of that already. Before you make any shifts or adjustments, try to make peace with the current state of your inner dialogue.

Take a few breaths to sit and observe your thoughts now. Do you notice any judgment, resistance, or urges to critique yourself or this process? Do you notice a desire for quick and easy change, to "fix" yourself, or skip ahead to get to the "real progress?" This is all your inner dialogue trying to convince you that you should be somewhere, anywhere, other than where you are. Ultimately, this is a way of resisting the feelings you are currently feeling, and denying your inner self the compassion needed to heal and grow.

Whatever you are feeling right now, and however your inner dialogue is treating you, know this. Your inner voice developed as a way to cope with your unique circumstances. It is another normal side-effect of being human. It can be molded and sculpted to better serve you as you move toward a more self-loving path. Accepting where you are now is the first and most crucial step toward creating this shift. Here are a few ways you can work to make peace with your inner voice:

Inner-Self Peace Offering Suggestions:
Take a moment to sit with your eyes closed and observe your thoughts. Acknowledge when they are positive and when they are negative. When they are negative, think the words, "I forgive you." When they are positive, think the words, "thank you."
Practice noticing when you are caught in self-critical thinking. Instead of continuing down that rabbit hole, invite yourself out for a walk instead.
Journal about the ways your negative inner dialogue has limited you or hurt you in the past. When you are done, write the words, "I accept this tendency as a part of who I am. I love myself as I am, and I am ready to shift to a more loving inner voice."

Little by little, you will start to believe these kind gestures and accept them. Continue practicing acceptance of who you are NOW, no matter how frustrated you get with yourself and the negative thoughts that creep back in. Stay curious and patient with yourself. Creating a peace offering, and repeatedly showing your inner self that you accept them for who they are, will slowly create the shift you are looking for. In this case, making peace does not mean remaining unchanged, because making peace is likely a new act for you. It's a vow to end the internal fight, letting your outer and inner selves work together, maybe for the first time. Stick with this, and you will begin to notice a shift toward a more forgiving and compassionate inner voice.

Shifting Toward Compassion

We may be more likely to critique the feminine parts of ourselves. This could be due to dynamics in childhood or ideas ingrained in us by society. There are plenty of outside forces that say certain parts of ourselves are simply "too much." After a while, we start to believe them, and attempt to shrink these parts of ourselves. Here are a few examples of feminine characteristics, those soft, intuitive, nurturing sides of ourselves, and how willing we are to view them as negative. I'll also include ways we can shift toward compassion by beginning to see these characteristics as vital parts of the whole.

Feminine quality:	We critique this quality as:	We can reclaim this quality by:
A desire for connection	Being too needy, clingy, or desperate for attention	Recognizing that human connection is vital, and we deserve to communicate our need for it without feeling judgment or shame.
Self-expression	Being too dramatic, stubborn, emotional, silly, annoying, or childish	Recognizing that creativity, play, and expression are fundamental elements of life. They help us learn, grow, and heal.
Intuition	Jumping to conclusions, being irrational, or being impulsive	Building self-trust, learning to acknowledge our inner voice, and making decisions that feel nurturing

Empathy	Being too sensitive, too serious, or being a people-pleaser	Acknowledging that empathy enriches our relationships when we maintain healthy boundaries surrounding our needs
Sensitivity	Being weak, too uptight, or too intense	Seeing sensitivity as an ability to feel everything life has to offer more fully; Taking emotional overwhelm as a cue to slow down and gain clarity
Generosity	Being a pleaser, over-sharing, giving too many chances, or not having strong boundaries	Maintaining healthy boundaries, and seeing generosity as a gift to those we love, as long as we are also offering it to ourselves

These are just a few examples of qualities you may see as "difficult to love" within yourself. When you view yourself as "too much," it becomes easy to dismiss your own needs, abandon your inner self, and avoid healing the pain you feel. As much as it may seem challenging to embrace certain aspects of who you are, sitting with the discomfort is a compassionate first step. Being willing to even acknowledge these characteristics is a sign that you are making a necessary internal shift toward kindness. Slowly, this compassionate inner voice will grow. Eventually, you'll recognize that carrying compassion with you makes life's difficult moments a bit less harsh. Maybe it will even make the good times a bit sweeter too.

Build a Flow of Kindness

That's the point in all of this. If you create a compassionate inner dialogue, one that reaches for kindness before criticism, you create a tool you can draw upon at any moment. It's an inner support system that helps you through hardship and celebrates your successes. You do this one moment at a time. You do this by journaling, taking time for a favorite hobby, going on a long hike, meditating, preparing a delicious meal for yourself, or however you prefer to check in. Check in, notice the quality of your thoughts, replace anything negative with a compassionate thought like, "You are doing your best, and that is good enough." Over time, these small steps build up and expand out into other areas of your life.

Maybe building a flow of inner kindness is the peace offering you've always needed. Maybe it still feels foreign and uncomfortable. Either way, lean in just to notice how you feel. Remember, before anything you read or attempt in this book, always consider your needs first. What would be the kindest gesture you could offer yourself right now?

Week 7 Daily Affirmations

This week's affirmations focus on that act of making a peace offering to your inner self. Use them to help you train your mind to shift out of judgment and into a place of kindness and compassion. Stay patient and know that no matter where you are in the process, you are building a loving support system within yourself.

"I am at peace with my inner voice. It protects me and showers me with love in each moment, and I am grateful."

"My truest self dwells within me. I offer this self persistent love and trust."

"Each time my inner dialogue becomes critical, I effortlessly shift toward a mindset of compassion."

"Kindness flows within me and expands out into every connection in my life."

"I see my inner self as a friend. I choose to make peace with every version of myself."

"I deserve to feel joy, regardless of my shortcomings. I deserve love, even if there are parts of myself I am still learning to love well."

"My inner world is a safe place for me to reside. I feel calm and at peace with myself."

Week 7 Healing Activities

1. **Kindness Meditation:** Sit down on a

comfortable, flat surface, and close your eyes. Begin to breathe fully in through your nose, and out through your mouth. Clasp your hands together gently and place them in your lap. Notice how it feels to hold your own hand. Notice any resistance you feel to this simple gesture. Continue to notice your breaths in and out. Think the words, "I am here for you." Imagine your clasped hands represent the connection of your inner and outer selves. Continue to sit in stillness, offering your inner self a moment of kindness for at least three minutes. Notice how this offering feels in your body.

2. **Action Step**: Write a few "kindness notes" for yourself, and stick them around your house. You can use the affirmations for this week, or create your own messages you think would lift your spirits throughout the day. Put them on your bathroom mirror, refrigerator, steering wheel, desk at work, or anywhere else you will see them often. Notice how these little gestures of kindness impact your mood.

3. **Peace Offering Self-hypnosis:** Read this script before you begin, making any adjustments you'd like to create a personal script for your recording. Once you've finished, record yourself saying the script slowly and clearly in an area with no background noise. Pause for at least ten seconds after each line of text to give yourself time for visualization. Lie down in a comfortable position, relax your body, and replay the recording.

"Take a deep breath and allow your hands to clasp together gently. Exhale and feel the warmth your hands begin to generate as they relax together.

As you breathe in, imagine you are sitting across from your inner self. Your inner self bows to you and you bow to them. You grow more and more relaxed as you accept the peace that is growing within you.

As your outer self and inner self radiate compassionate, kind energy between them, you begin to notice a warmth surrounding you.

This warmth is as powerful and bright as the sun. It embraces you fully. The kindness expressed within yourself has woken up more inner selves that are radiating acceptance and love.

You know that these selves represent you at each moment of your life, past, present, and future. You recognize that they are each offering unwavering kindness and compassion to you now.

The warmth expands out infinitely, and each of the infinite selves are embraced by its light. You know that these selves have infinite love and acceptance for you. You know that you can always turn inward and find their kindness radiating toward you.

You can access this inner compassion in any given moment. It joins you wherever you go, and you can tap into it as readily as feeling the warmth of the sun on your skin.

You are tapping into your own endlessly kind and compassionate inner voice. This voice is growing stronger and more confident in each moment. Each time you feel warmth you are reminded of this compassionate love inside of you.

Bring this warmth with you as you return back to consciousness. Wiggle your fingers and toes and slowly open your eyes. Tap into this kind and compassionate inner voice to make peace with yourself throughout the day."

Week 7 Reflection

1. Take some time to free-write your thoughts on how this week went. What did you enjoy? What was difficult? Which activities would you like to use again in the future?
2. Once you've reflected a bit about the week, come up with your own affirmation that sums up what you've learned about creating a compassionate inner voice. Try to pick a simple affirmation that can help you shift away from critical thinking and toward a place of kindness.

DID YOU ENJOY THIS BOOK?

We would truly appreciate if you could leave a review on Amazon. We are an independent publishing company and read each and every review!

amazon
★★★★★

Chapter 8

Build a Self-Image of Strength and Resilience

"And one has to understand that braveness is not the absence of fear but rather the strength to keep on going forward despite the fear."

Paulo Coelho (Goodreads, 2014)[9]

Think back to the last time you tried learning a new skill. Maybe this was something recent, or maybe your experiences in childhood come to mind, like learning to swim or ride a bicycle. You were starting from scratch, but you were likely hopeful that you would eventually master the skill. However, after hours of practice, trying and failing, falling and getting back up again, you started to feel like giving up. Whether you had someone helping you or you were learning on your own, someone had to convince you to persevere. That voice that told you not to give up, the voice that had faith in you despite your fears and struggles, is the reason that you kept going and eventually learned the skill.

Do you notice a tendency to want to give up when things are difficult?

Do you lose faith in yourself quickly, or have you learned to override thoughts that tell you you will not succeed?

If you have a sense of determination or faith in

yourself to succeed, what does that feel like? Does it feel like confidence, or does it feel like shaming yourself into performing at your best?

We all have some version of a self-image. This is as literal as what you see when you look in the mirror. It is also how you predict you will behave in certain situations, like how you think you will perform at work or when trying something new. Often, this self-image does play a role in predicting how we will perform. If the way we view ourselves is limiting, like not expecting ourselves to perform well under stress, we increase the likelihood that this prediction will come true. We can take a self-loving route by deciding to expand our self-image, to have a bit more confidence in the person we see in the mirror. When we create a self-image that incorporates confidence, strength, and resilience, we take a big step toward removing our inner roadblocks and opening up new doors for ourselves.

What is Your Self-Image?

We can have a self-image related to many different areas of life. Over time we develop a sense of what kind of friend, parent, sibling, partner, or worker we are. These images may be different relative to the area of life they encompass, but they likely have overarching similarities. If we have a generally positive view of ourselves, our self-image will likely be more positive. A negative inner dialogue may lend itself to a more negative self-image. We get so used to these ways that we view ourselves that we may not even notice them anymore. We begin to see this perception of ourselves as an undeniable truth. However, it may be beneficial to notice this tendency and get curious about where these thoughts are coming from. Let's take a look at a few questions you can ask yourself about your self-image.

Example of Self-Image Mistaken for Truth:	Non-judgmental Question for Getting Curious About this Thought:
"I am shy and lack confidence in social situations."	Is my shyness or lack of confidence really an effort to avoid putting myself out there?
"I procrastinate and tend to be lazy at work."	Is the thought that I am a procrastinator the reason I give in to procrastination? Do I procrastinate because I need more of a challenge, or because I have a fear that I will not succeed?
"When trying new things, I become frustrated quickly and give up easily."	Is my frustration because I feel that I am not good enough? If I viewed myself as good enough, would I be more willing to stick with difficult tasks?
"I am sensitive and defensive when receiving criticism."	Is my sensitivity rooted in the thought that criticism indicates that I am not worthy or capable?

"I am not feminine/ fashionable/ put-together/ attractive enough."	Whose standard am I judging myself by? Maybe embracing my body and my preferences regarding physical appearance would be a more loving approach?
"I cannot thrive in high-stress situations."	Are specific situations overwhelming to me because of the pressure I place on myself, or a lack of confidence in myself to succeed? Could I set up boundaries to take care of myself first, even in stressful situations?

Just like everything else we have discussed so far, your self-image is a natural product of your experiences in life and how you have responded to them. Every life experience, no matter how big or small, has been integrated into the perception you have of yourself. It is important to recognize a few things here. This is natural and happens to each of us. However, depending on a variety of factors, your self-image may not accurately represent who you are. If you mistake it for the truth, you place a number of limitations on how you operate in the world, and what you perceive yourself to be capable of. Recognizing this, you can begin shifting your self-image to a more positive place. You can realize that you already have more resilience and strength than you think. Not only will this shift your thinking process and expand your view of the possibilities in your life. It will also help you to worry less about the perceptions you believe other people have of you.

Restore Connections by Finding an Inner Friend

When we have negative thoughts about ourselves, we tend to expand them outward. We try to guess what other people think about us, and usually decide that their thoughts of us are also negative. Our self-image has this power to spread outside of ourselves and impact how we relate to the people around us. Here are a few ways negative self-image impacts our connections with the people in our lives:

- **We judge other people for the same reasons we judge ourselves.**
- **We gossip about other people to distract from our own insecurities.**
- **We assume everyone is judging and gossiping about us as well.**
- **We assume everyone's view of us is an exact replica of the negative ways we view ourselves.**
- **Interactions become defensive or distorted when we assume others see the worst in us.**
- **When we project our thoughts onto another person, we lose the ability to connect with them and really hear what they are saying.**

Do you see how clinging hard to a negative self-image can disrupt your connections with others? Unless we are judging others for the same reasons we judge ourselves, we often offer the people in our lives much more gentleness and grace than we give ourselves. Either way, this is an act of viewing ourselves as inferior to those around us. We forgive friends for their mistakes and understand when they are having an off day. We sit with them, give them a pep talk, and help them get to feeling better again. What would it be like if we offered this type of friendship to ourselves as well? What would it be like to see ourselves as just as deserving of kindness as the people we care about?

Viewing yourself as a friend reminds you to see the humanness in yourself again. It reminds you that an off day, a perceived weakness, or even a failure should not diminish the love you extend to yourself. Instead of attacking yourself and allowing your self-image to become more and more negative, you can offer yourself a pep talk. You can recognize that mistakes and fears are a part of life, and we don't need to read too much into them. Over time, this offering of friendship will help you remember your strength and bounce back quicker after setbacks.

The Courage to Rewrite Your Self-Image

Resilience is such an integral part of the human condition. When we fall, we get back up. Our bodies even know how to heal the scrapes and bruises we get along the way. If our bodies are such experts at healing wounds, do you think our minds are capable of a similar type of restoration?

The human mind is certainly complicated, but we do not have to be victims of the thinking styles that we have developed over time. If you view yourself in a negative light, or are hyper-critical when you make mistakes, know that you have the power to rewrite this tendency. These shifts take a bit of effort, and it may be useful to have a qualified professional help you get there. But even giving yourself this time to explore the ways you view yourself takes courage. Observing your own self-image, and acknowledging your power to build a new one, is a loving first step forward.

Take some time to think about what you want your self-image to be. Even if you don't believe these things about yourself just yet, exploring how you'd like to view yourself can provide great information as you work to rewrite your perception of yourself. Here are a few ideas for how you may want to view yourself. Create your own list, writing a few of these in a journal, or adding your own self-image goals:

Examples of Self-Image Goals:
"I am strong. I can handle criticism, stress, and hardship without questioning my own strength."
"I am confident in all social situations. I look after myself rather than attempting to please others."
"My sensitivity is an asset. My emotions are indicators of my needs. They help me connect more fully to myself and others."
"I can thrive in any situation I am faced with. If I find that I am struggling to thrive, I will protect myself rather than shaming myself."
"I am a hard worker, and I no longer allow fear or self-doubt to affect my performance."

Here's the thing. You deserve a self-image that creates possibilities rather than limitations. You deserve an inner space that is curious and friendly, and acknowledges the strength you already possess. You've made it to the end of chapter 8, so allow yourself to see the courage it has taken to stick with this process. The fact that you are here is indicative of the fact that you are beginning to see your worth. Whether or not you have fully embraced it, you are beginning to offer yourself genuine love. That alone is worth celebrating.

Week 8 Daily Affirmations

The affirmations for this week encourage you to acknowledge your internal strength and resilience. Use them as a focal point as you move toward a more positive self-image. Keeping these ideas in mind will remind you to be gentle and treat yourself as you would a friend. This offering of softness, kindness, and friendship will build a foundation for rewriting a positive and unwavering self-image of strength.

"I let criticism slide off my back. No one's opinion can change the love I feel for myself."

"Being human, making mistakes, and showing up again anyway is the ultimate act of courage."

"I trust myself to handle anything that comes my way with resilience and grace."

"I see myself as a sturdy force of love and strength."

"As I reveal my softness, my vulnerability, and my fears, I show up as my strongest self."

"There are lessons in both failure and success. Neither outcome affects my self-image because it is solid and unwavering."

"When I look in the mirror, I see someone who is trying to be better to themselves. I see that as the ultimate act of strength."

Week 8 Healing Activities

1. **Expansive Self-Image Meditation:** Sit down on a comfortable, flat surface and close your eyes. Begin to breathe fully in through your nose, and out through your mouth. Imagine there is a golden light surrounding you. As you breathe in, the light glows brighter. As you breathe out, it expands. You watch the light continue to expand and grow past the room you are in. It gets bigger and bigger until it is the size of your house, and then the size of your town, and then the size of your country. Soon, this light is bigger than the Earth itself. From your new perspective, everything in your life is small, and nothing can impact the size and the brightness of this light you have created. Continue to breathe in and out, noticing how it feels to have created such expansive energy, knowing that nothing can diminish it.

2. **Self-Image Goals Action Step**: Earlier in the chapter, you may have created a list of your self-image goals. If so, pull it out now. Choose one of the ways you wish to view yourself, and spend one day trying to embody this image. Notice the ways you embody this image with ease. Notice the moments that it is more difficult to continue embodying the image. If you want more confidence, maybe it is easy to be confident when walking down the street, but more difficult when you are chatting with your boss. Just notice these moments without judgment and write them down. This information will help you learn which types of situations affect your self-image the most. From there you can brainstorm ways to work toward maintaining a positive self-image, even when faced with difficult situations.

3. **Strong Self-Image Self-hypnosis:** Read this script before you begin, making any adjustments you'd like to create a personal script for your

recording. Once you've finished, record yourself saying the script slowly and clearly in an area with no background noise. Pause for at least ten seconds after each line of text to give yourself time for visualization. Lie down in a comfortable position, relax your body, and replay the recording.

"Breathe in and out, allowing a vibrant energy to wash over your body. You see this energy as strength and resilience, and accept them with ease as you settle in.

Breathe in, allowing this strength to wash over you. Breathe out, relaxing into the surface beneath you. You accept this vibrant energy, and allow it to calm you as you relax deeper.

You see your connection with the surface beneath you as the roots of a tree. They are growing deep down into the Earth now. They are solid and growing stronger with each breath. The energy and strength you feel effortlessly expand down into your roots, reaching deeper into the layers of the Earth.

Your body feels so relaxed and content now as you watch yourself sprout up like a tree. Your trunk thickens and grows taller and taller. You expand to take up more and more space, towering over the world around you.

You feel the strength you have inside of you emanating outward. This is an effortless sensation and it feels glorious.

You see yourself as this powerful, towering tree now. You know this unwavering strength is inside of you. You know you are a resilient being. This is the self-image you choose to see for yourself now.

You can access this sensation at any time. The deep, powerful roots, and the beautiful, towering strength are very much part of who you are. This is what you choose to see when you look in the mirror now.

This strong and resilient self-image is becoming easier and easier for you to tap into. You are doing such a good job of seeing yourself in this incredible new way. You are shifting your self-image so effortlessly now.

Let this vibrant energy trickle into your awareness as you slowly wiggle your fingers and toes. Open your eyes and carry this feeling with you as you stand up and continue your day."

Week 8 Reflection

1. Take some time to free-write your thoughts on how this week went. What did you enjoy? What was difficult? Which activities would you like to use again in the future?

2. Once you've reflected a bit about the week, come up with your own self-image affirmation that sums up what you've learned. Try to pick a simple affirmation that will offer gentleness and grace, while also helping you view yourself as strong.

Chapter 9

Celebrate Your Efforts and Bask in the Small Successes

"The journey of a thousand miles begins with a single step."

Lao Tzu (Goodreads, 2020)[10]

By now, you know that self-love isn't only found in the grand gestures in life. There is plenty of self-love to be found in ordinary, everyday tasks. Say you have needed a car wash for months. You keep putting it off because tasks at work, chores at home, and family activities continue to get in the way. This small task that will mostly only benefit you gets put on the back burner. Before you know it, it has been six months since you first realized you needed a car wash.

Are there any simple, mundane tasks in your life that you tend to put off?

If you know you feel so much better when these simple tasks are done, why do you put them off?

If you let yourself feel shame or guilt for not doing these things, do you also allow yourself to celebrate once you have gotten them done?

These little things like getting a car wash, trimming your

nails, or clearing out the junk drawer may seem unimportant, but they can have a big impact on how we view ourselves and our lives. Putting the things off that you know you need to do, especially when you are the main person who will benefit from the task being done, can begin to feel like self-neglect. The reminder that you still haven't done the task, like seeing your dirty car in the garage every day, sends a small dose of shame to your inner self. When we look at it this way, we can start to see that these tiny efforts do matter. They serve as a reminder that we aren't putting our own needs last anymore. As simple as it seems to clean out a junk drawer, it is also an act of self-love worthy of celebrating!

True Self-Celebration

There is great importance in celebrating yourself, your skills, your efforts, and even the smallest victories. When we reserve celebration for the big accomplishments, we send the message to ourselves that those are the only times worth celebrating.

Learning to celebrate the little things in life can play a crucial role in developing self-love.

Instead of hustling day after day, and only patting yourself on the back after a big achievement, why not build a bit of celebration into each day? Taking the time to appreciate yourself for the little things injects a bit of self-love into the ordinary tasks of our daily lives. Here are a few ideas for what celebrating yourself could look like:

Everyday Task You Normally Wouldn't Celebrate:	Idea for Celebrating this Simple Accomplishment:
You finally got a car wash.	Pick up a friend and go on a nice, long drive to catch up.
You cooked yourself a healthy meal.	Go on a stroll around the block to unwind and appreciate your body.

You cleaned out your junk drawer.	Add a bit of happiness to the space, like a photo of you and your family or a nice hand-written affirmation, to celebrate your organization and encourage you to keep it that way.
You did your taxes.	Create a gratitude journal to remind yourself of the good things that happened, even on stressful days.
You sat through a long, dull meeting at work.	Take a break before jumping back into work by doing some stretches, playing a round of ping pong, or going for a walk.

You don't have to throw yourself a party every time you do the dishes. These efforts of celebrating yourself can be as small as thinking one nice thought. We might normally tend to shame ourselves into a task like doing the dishes by thinking, "My house is a mess. I can't believe I let it get this bad!" Shifting this thought to, "I am doing the best I can, and I appreciate my effort to make my home a more comfortable place to be," turns the thought into an act of celebration. This kindness will make us a bit more optimistic about the monotonous tasks in life. We may even begin to get more joy out of ordinary things, rather than reserving our joy for the infrequent occurrence of a "big accomplishment."

The Little Things Are the Big Things

The sheer fact that there are so many small, seemingly insignificant tasks in life is reason enough to consider celebrating them. Each second passes by so quickly, but in the end, these seconds come together to create our memories and our life's story. Here are a few ways that celebrating the small moments in life can have a big impact:

- **Cultivate more presence during the ordinary activities in life.**
- **Observe your thoughts and begin to treat yourself better when completing simple tasks.**

- Learn what motivates you and apply the knowledge to increase your productivity.
- Move past limitations more easily and get tasks accomplished faster.
- Remove shame and guilt as primary motivators.
- Stop sabotaging your own daily routines by building a small reward into unpleasant activities.
- Add more joy, humor, and excitement into boring or stressful situations.
- Stop letting your negative thoughts impede your enjoyment throughout the day.
- Be gentle with yourself when you make mistakes or struggle to finish a task.
- Bounce back faster when you do encounter hurdles.

Getting more out of the little things will help you get more joy out of life. A little more joy, more satisfaction, more presence, and more authenticity will add up quickly. Life is a collection of billions of tiny, often boring, seemingly meaningless moments. Wouldn't celebrating these moments be another meaningful offering of self-love?

Make it a Habit!

Just like the other self-love practices we've discussed, self-celebration may not come naturally at first. When you are used to punishing and shaming yourself through your daily activities, you may need frequent reminders to shift into a positive mindset and stay there. But with patience, time, and persistence, celebrating yourself and finding joy in the little moments can become your new normal. Just as you developed your current coping strategies for getting through the monotonous moments of the day, you can work to develop new strategies that serve you better.

First, you'll want to figure out what motivates you. Do you get enjoyment out of catching up with friends, a physical activity, spending time alone journaling or meditating, or planning your next road trip? Learn your positive motivators and turn them into small moments of celebration throughout the day.

Next, you'll want to make a list of the celebration strategies you plan to use, and set reminders to act on them during the day. These activities should be very small, so they don't feel like another item on the to-do list. These may even be activities you would do during the day anyway, as a method of procrastination. Being intentional with these activities can help you eliminate that procrastination by consciously building celebration moments into your day. Here are some examples of how this could look:

Everyday Task:	Preferred Activity:	Incorporating an Intentional Celebration Habit:
Working on a tedious data-entry project at work	Doing yoga	Set an alarm for one hour of work. Once you've finished the hour, take a break to do some stretches!

Cleaning the floors in your house	Catching up with friends	When you've cleaned half of the floors, take a break to send a friend a voice message or text to catch up!
Organizing your home	Going for a walk	After completing a chunk of the organization, or finishing one task, go for a short walk to clear your mind before continuing with other tasks!
Waiting on the phone with customer service	Planning a trip	While waiting on the phone, make a list of places you want to go or things you need to do to plan the trip. After you've finished the call, celebrate by completing one task on the trip to-do list!

Of course, these habits will look different for everyone. The important thing is exploring which tasks you dread, and which you love, and realize that you can use this information to your advantage! Instead of working against yourself by procrastinating, and shaming yourself for procrastination, you can learn to power through the dull moments and reward yourself with the activities you love! This is a simple yet important way that you can start working in communion with your own needs. Learn that you deserve to set aside time to celebrate yourself every day. Making this a habit is another powerful act of self-love.

Small Steps, Big Impact

By now, I hope you've realized that the time to celebrate is now. You are almost at the finish line of this self-love exploration, but the journey doesn't end here. The small steps and tiny adjustments you have made over the past nine weeks have come together to mean much more. You've gotten curious, stayed patient, and observed the steps that work best for you. You've stuck with this journey when you were met with difficulty, discomfort, and resistance. You may still feel far away from the idea of self-love, but the steps you've taken have all been loving. This is where you come to embody self-love. This is why small, persistent, daily steps are so worth celebrating. When we see the tiny moments of our lives as valuable, we realize that it is in these moments that we can heal, grow, and practice treating ourselves a bit kinder.

Week 9 Daily Affirmations

This week's affirmations focus on the act of caring for and appreciating yourself in each moment. The act of celebrating yourself reminds you that you have your own back no matter what. Whether you are working on an important project or simply doing the dishes, celebrating yourself adds moments of awareness and self-love into your day. Use these affirmations to remind yourself that celebration should not just be reserved for big achievements. Instead, celebrate the ordinary, and watch how this transforms your days.

"I am learning to notice the moments when I choose to take care of myself."

"I celebrate the little things. I am always looking out for me."

"I celebrate myself every day."

"My true self is showing up more and more every day."

"My habits reflect an effort to love myself more and more."

"I am starting to notice a shift in my internal dialogue. I more readily act out of self-love rather than guilt or judgment."

"Every day, I give myself the kind of love and celebration I used to believe was reserved for special occasions."

Week 9 Healing Activities

1. **Morning Celebration Meditation:** Sit down on a comfortable, flat surface, and close your eyes. Begin to breathe fully in through your nose, and out through your mouth. Envision how you want your day to go. Watch the day pass exactly how you want it to. You exude confidence in each activity, and you fully enjoy each moment. Now, envision how you will feel at the end of the day. Feel a warm light come over you as you acknowledge that you worked as hard as you could, appreciated each moment, and made the most of even the smallest tasks. Allow yourself to sit for a few minutes in this warm light, celebrating this great day, knowing that everything is exactly as it should be.

2. **Action Step**: Treating yourself to something nice, just for the sake of it, may feel a bit foreign at first. We are going to practice rewarding ourselves just for being wherever we are on this

journey toward cultivating self-love. Today, treat yourself to your favorite warm beverage in a nice, cozy chair. If it is summer, grab a nice refreshing drink and a seat in the sun. Do not bring your phone or any other distractions. Just sit and enjoy, noticing thoughts that come up and returning to the present. Try to sit and enjoy for at least six minutes.

3. **Celebration Self-hypnosis:** Read this script before you begin, making any adjustments you'd like to create a personal script for your recording. Once you've finished, record yourself saying the script slowly and clearly in an area with no background noise. Pause for at least ten seconds after each line of text to give yourself time for visualization. Lie down in a comfortable position, relax your body, and replay the recording.

"Close your eyes, and breathe in and out calmly. You settle in easily and return to this familiar state of peace. You do this as easily as your breath comes in and goes out.

As you breathe in, you notice an overwhelming sense of joy within you. You breathe out and notice all muscle tension easily melting away.

As you relax more deeply now, you notice you are up on a stage. You feel a gentle breeze gliding along your skin as you calmly peer out in front of you.

Your body feels so relaxed now. You breathe in and out, noticing there is a sea of your favorite people surrounding you in the crowd below. You see your inner self stand up and begin to applaud you.

You feel your body relax as you accept the love that your loved ones, and yourself, extend to you now. You are completely relaxed as you allow joy to spread through every inch of your body.

You allow the emotion and joy to well up as you acknowledge how hard you have worked. You accept this feeling of accepting unconditional love and support coming from yourself and your loved ones.

You feel as if you are floating. Your mind and body are calm and welcome this celebration so readily. You know that you can tap into this feeling at any time.

You are welcoming celebration for your efforts in life with more ease every day. You allow yourself to feel this joy, contentment, and peace growing stronger and stronger.

Welcome yourself back to awareness with a smile. You have earned a bit of celebration for your efforts. You continue to offer yourself this energy as you continue with your day."

Week 9 Reflection

1. Take some time to free-write your thoughts on how this week went. What did you enjoy? What was difficult? Which activities would you like to use again in the future?

2. Once you've reflected a bit about the week,

come up with your own self-celebration affirmation that sums up what you've learned. Try to pick a simple affirmation that can help you get more enjoyment out of the small, everyday tasks in life.

Chapter 10

Breathe Self-Love into Your Routines Moving Forward

*"Your beliefs become your thoughts,
Your thoughts become your words,
Your words become your actions,
Your actions become your habits,
Your habits become your values,
Your values become your destiny."*

Mahatma Gandhi (Goodreads, 2020)[11]

Now that we've spent several weeks exploring different facets of self-love, you may have already begun incorporating a few self-love practices into your daily routines. Say you're trying to revolutionize your morning routine. You decide you need to wake up two hours earlier than normal, meditate for ten minutes, do yoga for thirty minutes, take a shower, and cook a hot breakfast. The first week you do pretty well, but soon you notice it is difficult to keep up with this goal. Normally you would force yourself to push through with these habits and shame yourself for falling short. However, after exploring self-love a bit, you decide to question this approach.

When creating routines, do you leave a bit of wiggle room for life's inevitable complications?

Does the failure to stick to a new routine cause you to slip out of it altogether?

What do you think a self-loving approach to routines would look like?

When getting curious about your routines, it helps to take a look at your motivators. What are your core reasons for carrying out the routines you've established in your life? Maybe your routines are a result of operating in auto-pilot, and you aren't really sure why you do them. Maybe you guilt-trip yourself into routines that seem healthy on the outside. Maybe your routines truly are continual acts of self-love. Getting to the root of these motivators can help you build routines that feel more achievable, and more loving, in the long-run.

Explore Your Routines

Whether you intentionally created them or not, you already have routines in your life. We may go through the motions of the routines in our lives without questioning why we do the things we do. As we discussed last week, the routines in our lives are another example of seemingly meaningless actions that we can choose to enjoy a bit more. You can learn to care about your routines and honor yourself when completing these actions. Becoming mindful of the way you carry out routines is an act of self-love. When you bring self-love into your routines, you can ensure that you stick with your loving practices, even when you feel busy or overwhelmed. Examine your routines by asking the following questions:

- **Did I intentionally create my routines, or are they made up of actions I do unconsciously?**

- **Does my morning routine set me up for success or leave my feeling stressed out?**

- **Does my evening routine leave my mind rattled and make it difficult to fall asleep, or does it help me relax and unwind both mentally and physically?**

- **Do I have moments in my routines where I am aware, present, and at ease?**

- **Are my routines put in place to force myself into more productivity, or do they include caring efforts to take care of my body and mind?**

Use the questions to gain a bit of awareness regarding your daily routines, but don't get the idea that you need to do a complete routine overhaul. Maybe you're realizing that a lot of your routines could be serving you better, or you spend a good portion of your day in autopilot. Accept this and allow it. If we decide we need to completely redesign our entire lives, we will quickly become overwhelmed and feel like we are failing. This will bring up the shame and guilt tendency we have been trying to undo. The key here is to acknowledge that where you are and where you want to be may be two different places, and that's okay. Your present self still deserves appreciation. Find self-love in taking baby steps and staying consistent with them. Over time, you'll slowly build the momentum needed to create the routines you want.

Weave an Element of Self-Love

So, self-love is in the small gestures, right? But what does this mean, and how do we actually take these steps? These answers will largely depend on you and your goals. But first, consider the idea that it is loving to be gentle with yourself. It is loving to realize that humans need time to change. If you do want to overhaul your routines, it is loving to realize that a significant amount of change will not happen right away. There is love to be found in deciding on one or two daily practices to begin implementing into your daily routine. After a week of consistently completing these steps, you can decide if you are ready to add one more. Your inner self will see these efforts of showing up every single day. Like a child, your inner self will learn, through your actions, that you love yourself.

Here are a few ideas for self-loving routines you can implement at different times of the day. Again, I would recommend choosing one or two to start. Focus on routines that make you feel calm, present, and nurtured in both your mind and body. Maybe start with one new routine in the morning, and another in the evening, and work your way up from there.

Time of Day:	Self-loving Routine Ideas to Incorporate:
Morning: **Before choosing, ask yourself, "Is this achievable and enjoyable?"**	• Meditate for five to ten minutes • Write one page in your journal to check in with yourself mentally • Take five minutes to stretch to check in with yourself physically • Make yourself a warm beverage and take five minutes to enjoy it without screens • Go on a ten-minute walk to energize your body and mind
Commute to work: **Before choosing, ask yourself, "Is this shifting me toward autopilot or awareness?"**	• Check in with your body and your senses. What do you notice about the sights, sounds, and feelings around you? • Listen to a podcast on a topic that excites you • Focus on taking full breaths, and returning to your breath when distracting thoughts come up

Breaks throughout the workday: **Before choosing, ask yourself, "What action would tell my inner self I appreciate their hard work?"**	• Get up to stretch or take a five-minute walk every hour • Take a moment to journal to leave your distracting thoughts on the paper • Make yourself a warm beverage • Take a five-minute meditation break • Take five minutes to research a topic that interests you. Set a timer so you don't spend too much time.
After work: **Before choosing, ask yourself, "What would help me transition from work into a more relaxed mindset?"**	• Change clothes right away and do ten minutes of physical activity • Make yourself and a loved one a snack to enjoy together • Set an alarm to do ten minutes of tidying up • Take ten minutes with no screens, outside if possible

Evening:	• Have a designated time when all screens turn off, preferably two hours before bed
Before choosing, ask yourself, "What would put my mind at ease and help my body relax for sleep?"	• Get in bed half an hour before you want to go to sleep, and spend the extra time reading or meditating
	• Pay attention to your senses by putting on comfortable clothes, dimming the lights, and turning off any noisy gadgets
	• Stretch your legs or rub them with a soothing lotion

Self-loving routines allow you to remind yourself that you are loved, without parting from the necessary tasks of your day. You do not need to go on a retreat to weave a tiny amount of self-love into your day. These little efforts of tuning into your body and senses, cultivating presence in your mind, and repeating these steps daily will help you heal and learn to trust yourself. Once you discover activities you adore, repeating them each day will become effortless, yet still remain a meaningful act of self-love.

Acknowledge the Role of Society

Any resistance we feel when incorporating self-love practices may come from what we have learned from society. Society tells us to work harder than expected, turn hobbies into side-hustles, change our bodies, be funnier or more social, be quieter or more mature, and the list goes on. At some point, these external messages become our internal voice, and we learn to tell ourselves over and over again that we need to be different than we are.

This is why consistent self-loving practices are so important. If these messages to question our worth or shame ourselves are so constant, our efforts to shift out of that mindset should also be constant. Practicing self-love reminds you that you deserve acceptance as you are. It helps you to gently push back against the unconscious factors that convince us to judge ourselves or mentally tune out altogether. Remember that your self-love practice is powerful in this sense. As you push back against the feeling that you are undeserving, unworthy, incapable, or flawed, you push yourself toward healing, reconnecting with your inner self, and reconnecting with your loved ones and your community. This effort is not selfish, but vital.

Check in and Maintain Your Efforts

Once you find the ways you enjoy incorporating self-love into your routines, come up with a method for checking in to make sure you are sticking with them. This will be a way you can hold yourself accountable, without pushing yourself too hard or judging yourself when you need to skip a day. Here are a few ideas for self-love check-ins.

- **Have a daily self-love journal entry. Write a couple of lines describing your self-love practice for the day and how it made you feel.**

- **Draw a heart on your calendar after finishing your self-love practice for the day.**

- **Put a sticky note on your mirror or in your workspace, and write a tally mark once you've done your self-love practice for the day.**

- **Set a reminder to check in at the end of each month to write about how your self-love activities went, and how you may want to adjust them for next month.**

The bottom line is, daily self-love matters. But don't forget that some days, self-love may come in the form of forgiving yourself for skipping an activity or slipping up somehow. Return to this idea of showing yourself love, and how it might look different each week, each day, and even each moment. Slowly you'll start to strengthen your inclination toward self-love, and it will become a reflex. You may still have negative thoughts or feelings toward yourself, but you'll be able to shift out of them quicker, and into a more loving place.

Week 10 Daily Affirmations

This week's affirmations remind you to be intentional when creating loving daily routines. They encourage you to see the effort of creating loving routines as an easy and natural process. Use these affirmations to remember that you are creating these routines to treat yourself well. Regardless of your achievements each day, self-love should be the overarching motivator behind your efforts.

"My routines reflect an inner sentiment of self-love."

"I maintain healthy routines with ease because the driving motivator is taking care of myself."

"I am beginning to infuse self-love into every routine in my life. This process feels as easy as breathing."

"I build new routines with ease."

"I honor myself in the routines I create. I check in regularly to make sure they are still serving me well."

"I observe my thoughts to make sure my actions are fueled by a loving and nurturing mindset."

"I make adjustments to my routines effortlessly and without judgment."

Week 10 Healing Activities

1. **Calming Evening Meditation:** Sit or lie down on a comfortable, flat surface and close your eyes. Begin to breathe fully in through your nose, and out through your mouth. Imagine there is a calming lavender colored cloud hovering over your feet. The cloud makes your feet feel extremely heavy and relaxed. Your feet are still and ready to rest for the evening. Allow this cloud to work its way up your body, making your legs, hips, torso, arms, neck, eyelids, and head feel extremely heavy. Eventually, the cloud covers your entire body. Your breath becomes

even slower, and you resign to a restful, peaceful state. As you come back to awareness, you watch the cloud drift away, taking all of your remaining energy with it, and leaving you to sleep your soundest sleep.

2. **Action Step**: This week, pick one or two self-loving efforts that you would like to add to your daily routine. This week, do these new routines every day. Make a journal entry for the seven days to document your progress. In these entries, free write how the activities are going for you. Afterward, answer the following questions:
   - **Are these new routines adding more self-love into my life?**
   - **Are these routines affecting my thoughts throughout the day?**
   - **Do these routines feel difficult or easy? Do I notice any resistance to self-love?**
   - **If these routines are not working, how can I adjust them to make them feel more achievable, or more "me?"**

3. **Self-Love Embodying Hypnosis:** Read this script before you begin, making any adjustments you'd like to create a personal script for your recording. Once you've finished, record yourself saying the script slowly and clearly in an area with no background noise. Pause for at least ten seconds after each line of text, to give yourself time for visualization. Lie down in a comfortable position, relax your body, and replay the recording.

"Breathe in and out, coming to the present with ease, and blinking your eyes until they grow heavy.

As you breathe in, pay attention to any physical sensations you feel. As you breathe out, let go of the sensations and drop into a state of total peace.

As you relax deeper and deeper, you are greeted by your inner self. This familiar friend sits next to you, and you continue to breathe effortlessly.
Your body feels so relaxed and content now. You are drifting deeper and deeper into relaxation. You notice your inner and outer selves begin to merge together as

one. This feels like a natural and kind gesture of love. You continue to sink deeper and deeper together.

This union happens as naturally as gravity holds you to the Earth. You accept your inner and outer selves and offer them love so easily now.

I am coming into communion with my inner and outer selves so effortlessly now. This process feels like love. Loving myself feels as easy as floating in a warm bath.

I know my self-love practice is yielding powerful results. I am showing up for myself every day as an act of unconditional love. I feel this sensation at all moments of each day. If I lose the feeling, it quickly comes back as I float back to awareness.

I offer myself love, acceptance, kindness, and trust. I offer these things subconsciously, and with total ease.

I offer myself unconditional love, acceptance, kindness, and trust as I shift back to awareness now. Each time I shift back to awareness, this feeling of self-love comes flooding back to me.

I wiggle my fingers and toes and open my eyes now. I continue to offer myself this love as I continue through my routines, and return to this feeling readily throughout each day."

Week 10 Reflection

1. Take some time to free-write your thoughts on how this week went. What did you enjoy? What was difficult? Which activities would you like to use again in the future?

2. Once you've reflected a bit about the week, come up with your own affirmation that sums up what you've learned about maintaining self-love routines in your daily life. Try to pick a simple affirmation that can remind you of the importance of maintaining your self-love practices every day.

Conclusion

Tying it All Together

"There is a candle in your heart,
ready to be kindled.
There is a void in your soul, ready to be filled.
You feel it, don't you?"

Rumi (Goodreads, 2020)[12]

You've made it to the end of this self-love journey! Congratulations! Hopefully by now you have realized a few things about the concept of self-love:

Self-love isn't:	Self-love is:
...an isolated action that you do once and then you are "healed forever!"	...a life long practice that requires a bit of daily action and a lot of self-acceptance.
...required in order for you to give or receive love from others.	...knowing you are worthy of love no matter how much you may struggle to love yourself on any given day.
...a selfish act that takes away from the other connections in your life.	...a necessary act that adds richness and depth to the other connections in your life.
..always as easy as bubble baths and a movie night.	..difficult on some days, but the real love comes from not giving up on yourself in the difficult moments.
...something to shame or guilt yourself into doing.	...something to practice with a mindset of acceptance and ease.
...something that we will have in the future.	...something we have the ability to practice at each moment.

Remember, you deserve love and *are* loved, no matter how you feel at the end of this book. Staying patient and making it to the end of this book was a giant leap toward loving yourself a little bit more every day. This is a practice worthy of your time and energy. By taking this time for yourself, you've shown your inner self that they are worth that time and energy too.

Now that you know you can practice self-love at any moment, I hope you are ending this book with hope for a more loving and kind future. Even if you are still working toward loving yourself better, you have come a long way just by staying persistent, exploring affirmations and hypnosis, and chipping away at the weekly activities and prompts.

Revisiting Our Promises

It's important to revisit the promises we made in the beginning, to recognize just how far we have come on this journey. Do you remember my promise to you at the beginning of this book? Let's revisit it now:

> *"My promise to you is that if you begin this journey from a place of curiosity, kindness, and openness, you will trigger the shift necessary to access a self-love practice."*

I hope you were able to adjust into your self-love practice with ease. However, if you experienced resistance along the way, know that this is normal. Finishing this book is a testament to the fact that you overcame the obstacles, and you still showed up to love yourself anyway. Continue to operate with curiosity, kindness, and openness. Continue to shift out of resistance and judgment, and return back to self-love once again.

What was your promise to yourself? See if you can find where you wrote it down now. Did working toward this promise help you build a more loving relationship with yourself? If the promise didn't work out as planned, were you gentle and forgiving toward yourself anyway? Regardless of how things unfolded, these promises are worth remembering as you continue your self-love practice outside of this book.

Self-Love, Now

Over the course of this book, you've explored the ways you can connect with yourself to begin healing your body and mind. Let's take a look at the topics we've covered over the course of this book.

Finding awareness in the present
Taking care of yourself
Embracing vulnerability
Honoring your authenticity
Building self-trust
Allowing yourself to rest
Cultivating an inner kindness
Constructing a resilient self-image
Celebrating yourself
Maintaining self-loving, consistent routines

These ideas are all central to living in a self-loving way, but they will not always come naturally. Whether you read this book in a few weeks or over the course of a year, you may still find yourself wrestling with a few of these concepts. You may find that some days you are not capable of a single item on this list. And that's okay! The important thing is that you've learned that you can love yourself anyway. It's a great goal to become a self-love guru, but it's arguably even more impressive to acknowledge the difficulty in this practice. Real self-love shows up when you accept yourself, inner demons and all, and continue to offer yourself love anyway. That's what we've started to uncover, and that will be your work moving forward.

Let the Feminine Be

How have you treated the feminine sides of yourself during this process? How has your idea of what it means to be feminine shifted? Every human has feminine qualities. Some of us show them openly, and some suppress them for fear of being perceived as weak or emotional. These elements, such as gentleness, care, intuition, emotion, generosity, wisdom, openness, and vulnerability are difficult to reveal, because they make us feel exposed and raw. We feel others will judge us for showing these sides of ourselves. Hopefully, you've learned to begin embracing these parts of yourself, rather than hiding or fighting them. Doing so is an act of courage. A peace-offering to yourself.

Allowing each part of you, feminine, masculine, neutral, or otherwise, to just be, creates a sense of ease, don't you think? You do not need to be different than you are, and I hope this book has helped you see that. You don't need to hide your emotions, feelings, or whatever else you feel others will dislike about you. Feminine energy is all about being and allowing. Be who you are, and allow that to be enough.

Where to Go From Here

Know that no matter what, this exploration of self-love found you when it was meant to. You may not have been a self-love master before, and you may not be now. In fact, hopefully, now you know that it doesn't even work that way. Self-love isn't something to master, earn a certificate of completion, and move on forever. Self-love is in daily acts of showing up to care for yourself. Self-love is in shifting out of negative thoughts when you feel them creep in. Self-love is acknowledging that you deserve to be treated well, no matter how hopeless you may feel.

In your efforts of meditation, self-hypnosis, journaling, and other action steps, you've begun to form these self-loving habits. Everything you've discovered during these practices is useful information you can use to grow and adjust your personal self-love practices. Continue the daily habits that helped you, and leave behind the ones that didn't fit quite right. The biggest takeaway is knowing that you are worth the time and energy you have put in. You are worth continuing to fine-tune your self-love practice each day, for the rest of your days.

Ending with a Promise

What do you plan to do to continue working on self-love? Take some time to journal about this as your time with this book comes to a close. You can come back to this book whenever you want, but you have the skills necessary to build and maintain your own unique self-love practice. Write down one promise you plan to keep in the days, weeks, months, and years to come. Let this be your first affirmation as you continue on this next step of your journey. As always, I will close with my promise to you.

My promise to you is that you have always had inherent worth, value, and strength. You have always deserved kindness, care, trust, and love. Moving forward with this knowledge, your self-love practice will help you build a deeper relationship with yourself, and the world around you, than you ever imagined."

Here are a few promises you may consider making to yourself now:

- I promise to continue five minutes of self-love journaling every day.
- I promise to continue the meditation and hypnosis practices three days a week.
- I promise to meditate on one self-love affirmation once a week.
- I promise to connect with my inner self through a daily afternoon stroll.
- I promise to adjust my self-love practice daily as it feels appropriate for my body and mind.
- I promise to be a little bit kinder to myself today.
- I promise to do one thing right now that is self-loving.

Once you have decided on a promise, smile, put your hand on your heart, and thank yourself for this effort you have made. Take a moment to acknowledge your progress with a full breath in and out.

Now, close this book and continue your journey, one self-loving step at a time.

Resources

(1) Berry, W., & Meatyard, R. E. (2006). *The Unforeseen Wilderness: Kentucky's Red River Gorge*. Emeryville, CA: Shoemaker Hoard.

(2) A quote by Mother Teresa. (n.d.). Retrieved January 10, 2020, from https://www.goodreads.com/quotes/44552-yesterday-is-gone-tomorrow-has-not-yet-come-we-have

(3) Nhat Hạnh Thich. (2011). *Reconciliation: Healing the Inner Child*. Berkeley, CA: Parallax.

(4) Brown Brené. (2015). *Daring Greatly: How the Courage to be Vulnerable Transforms the Way We Live, Love, Parent, and Lead*. London, England: Penguin Books Ltd.

(5) Tolle, E. (2018). *A New Earth: Awakening to Your Life's Purpose*. London: Penguin Books.

(6) Oliver, M. (2017). *Devotions: the Selected Poems of Mary Oliver.* New York: Penguin Press, an imprint of Penguin Random House LLC.

(7) Angelou, M. (2002). *Wouldn't Take Nothing for My Journey Now.* New York: Random House.

(8) Hay, L. (2017). *You Can Heal Your Life.* Place of publication not identified: Hay House Inc.

(9) A quote by Paulo Coelho. (n.d.). Retrieved February 10, 2020, from https://www.goodreads.com/quotes/94972-and-one-has-to-understand-that-braveness-is-not-the

(10) A quote by Lao Tzu. (n.d.). Retrieved February 23, 2020, from https://www.goodreads.com/quotes/21535-the-journey-of-a-thousand-miles-begins-with-a-single

(11) A quote by Mahatma Gandhi. (n.d.). Retrieved February 28, 2020, from https://www.goodreads.com/quotes/50584-your-beliefs-become-your-thoughts-your-thoughts-become-your-words

(12) A quote by Rumi. (n.d.). Retrieved March 6, 2020, from https://www.goodreads.com/quotes/78367-there-is-a-candle-in-your-heart-ready-to-be

Hello, it's Confidence Calling!

A Self-Confidence and Self-Esteem Workbook for Women

Overcome shyness, self-doubt, and anxiety for good!

Written by: Elena Wright

Table of Contents

Introduction 217

Chapter 1 - Discover self-confidence and
              why it's worth developing 229
    What is self-confidence? 230
    What is self-esteem? 233
    Why is self-confidence so important?..236
    Small steps you can take right now to improve your
    self-confidence 240
    Start your 30-day Recovery Plan Activities................................241
    Day 1-3 of your 30-day Recovery Plan......................................243

Chapter 2 - Observe Your Present Self to Move
              Forward without Judgment..................247
    Observing your current state of confidence..............................248
    9 Common Signs that your confidence is dipping......................252
    Making Judgments..254
    Does my self-esteem stem from my childhood? 256
    The Psychology of Self-Confidence 258
    What different behaviors suggest low self-esteem?..................261
    How quickly can I improve my self-esteem? 272
    Days 4-6 of your 30-day Recovery Plan....................................273

Chapter 3 - Tackle Shyness to Present Your
              Authenticity in Any Crowd 277

What is shyness, how it develops and ways to move past it?...278
What's the difference between shyness and introversion?.......280
Social anxiety and Shyness 283
Staying Authentic 284
Day 7-9 of your 30-day Recovery Plan 288

Chapter 4 - Move from Self-Doubt into Self-Trust to Solidify Your Internal Relationship..291

Where does self-doubt come from? 292
Where does imposter syndrome come from? 294
What are self-limiting beliefs and how do we overcome them? .296
How can I start to trust myself and instill self-belief? 299
Self-doubt versus living with solid self-trust..............................302
Day 10-12 of your 30-day Recovery Plan..................................304

Chapter 5 - Soothe Anxiety and Learn to "Recharge" Your Confidence 307

How symptoms of anxiety could be knocking your confidence ...308
Effective rest and stress-relief strategies that help you control your anxieties 312
How can resting and taking care of myself help my confidence?...315
How can I make changes to boost my energy levels? 317
Day 13-15 of your 30-Day Recovery Plan 320

Chapter 6 - Check Your Self-Image to Eliminate Tendencies of Comparison 325

What do we mean by 'self', what is self-image, and how is it formed and developed? 326

How comparing ourselves makes us unhappy and
gives our confidence a bashing 332
Self-esteem and confidence in a digital age 336
Day 16-18 of your 30-day recovery plan 339

Chapter 7 - Uncover the Negative Stories You Tell Yourself to Rewrite Your Inner Dialogue..343

We all have a story to tell our self, but how accurate are they? 344
How important are our internal stories?....................................346
How to observe your inner dialogue and rewrite it 349
Day 19-21 of your 30-day Recovery Plan 353

Chapter 8 - Build Self-Care Routines that Remind You of Your Worth 357

Self-care and why we need it 358
How to boost your self-worth 361
Feeling well-cared for versus feeling worthy 364
Are hobbies a type of self-care? 367
Days 22-24 of your 30-day Recovery Plan 368

Chapter 9 - Observe Improvements You've Made to Start Giving Yourself Credit for Progress 371

Big goals versus small goals 373
What if I don't know I've achieved something? 377
How should I celebrate my success? 380
Days 25-27 of your 30-day Recovery Plan 383

Chapter 10 - Establish Actions to Move Forward into a Life of Exuding with Confidence 385

Retaining confidence, even if there are setbacks 386
Establish a daily routine that boosts your
confidence and self-esteem 389
7 Tips to bounce back faster when you make mistakes 394
Negative emotions and how to deal with them 396
How to develop your resilience 398
Maintaining your ideal level of confidence and self-esteem 399
Days 28-30 of your 30-day Recovery Plan 402
Moving Forward... 403

Conclusion 407

Reference List 415

Introduction

"As soon as you trust yourself, you will know how to live."

Johann Wolfgang von Goethe

Do you trust your own actions and abilities? According to Johann Wolfgang von Goethe above, it's only then you can start to live your life. If you don't trust yourself to do something, how can you expect others to trust you? In life, people want you to make guarantees and assurances that you 'can', not that you 'might or think you can', especially in a professional capacity. It's difficult to suggest that you can certainly do something if you don't have that self-belief and self-worth.

As women we go through life comparing ourselves. We compare ourselves to other models in magazines, we compare ourselves to other wives and mothers, and we compare our careers, education and relationships. We want to be the best at everything, some women even want to be the best cook and compare themselves to others. Imagine a child going home after a playdate and telling her mom that the other kids mom makes the *best* cupcakes. Something like that can be a slap in the face but ultimately, if you feel threatened or upset by this comment, it's you who needs to change. Making nicer cupcakes does not make the other mom a better mother than you, nor does it make her a better cook. If those thoughts enter a person's mind – this is you doubting yourself and your mind processing this all wrong, because firstly, kids sometimes say some funny things they don't mean. They often exaggerate and it was probably a compliment because they had a great time. Next, that might be the only sweet thing your child has eaten today, and it was a treat, and finally, we all have different likes and dislikes; plus, we simply can't be the best at everything. This needs to be reframed – Sally's Mom (the other mom) makes good cakes, it's her strength. Also, your child just had a lovely time visiting her friend, so above all, this is a time for joy! Processing small events like this in an irrational way can damage your self-confidence, and this is something that some of us do on a regular basis, unknowingly.

Self-confidence and self-esteem are complex. They are a state of mind that attempt to define our thoughts and feelings, but they are difficult to control because they focus on ourselves. It is often difficult to see our own qualities, trust our own abilities, and to feel like we've made the best judgment call. We might even think about what we could've done, should've done, or would've done in certain situations, and we tend to beat ourselves up about it because we feel like we just didn't handle things well. *Does this sound familiar?* That is your self-doubt niggling away at you and it's bringing down your confidence, just like the cupcake example from earlier.

These feelings can affect us because the way we feel about ourselves often shapes the way we think and behave. If we feel like we're not good enough, this shows. How can we expect others to have faith in us, or believe we can do something, if we don't believe it of ourselves? Confident people are comfortable in their own skin but for someone who lacks confidence, this doesn't come naturally and for many people this rings a familiar sound of self-doubt.

Self-confidence and self-esteem can either be your best friend, or your worst enemy. If we allow it to control us in a negative way, it can affect everything we do. If we control it positively, we can rule the world and inspire others. Confidence can truly be the determining factor in what we do next in our life because it can mean success, or it can scupper our dreams. It influences the decisions we make in our personal lives, relationships, careers, and education.

Imagine you approach two self-confidence coaches to find out what they can do for you. You explain your situation and the first one says:

'I think I might be to help you to improve your confidence and self-esteem.'

The second tells you:
'I can help you to improve your confidence and self-esteem.'

Which one would you choose?

A coach costs a lot of money so most people wouldn't take a chance on someone who *might be able to* help them – they want someone who *can.* In order for that coach to say she CAN help, she shows one important thing; confidence in her own abilities! *How can someone teach you to be confident if they are not confident themselves?*

You're right, they can't and that's exactly why you would need a coach who believes in themselves to get the results you require.

Lacking in confidence can hold us back in life because we often end up doing things we don't want to do.

Maybe we were too shy to tell the boss that we couldn't work over tonight, so now we've agreed to it and now we feel anxious because we've had to arrange for someone to pick our kids up from school. Maybe we couldn't speak out about something because we felt so anxious and were afraid we'd make a fool of ourselves. We then spend so much time reflecting on these events, beating ourselves up because we didn't say no or handle it differently and this sets off all kinds of negative emotions. We regret that we didn't react differently.

As human beings, we don't like to have regrets. We have this idea of perfectionism in our head and anything less just isn't good enough. In reality, we set the standard so high that we are never going to be 'perfect' and by aiming for this, we are setting ourselves up for disappointment. Perfectionism is often part of the problem, because nobody is perfect.

Imagine you're at a conference and this amazing woman enters the speaking area. She looks happy, walks confidently, and she speaks so well, with ease, and it's like she's talking directly to you. She speaks to people at the reception afterwards and she is the ultimate socialite. You aspire to be her...

What if I told you that inside, just before the event, she was terrified? That a few years ago, she wouldn't have even attempted to board a stage or speak in front of so many people. A year ago, she was shy and anxious, and constantly beating herself up about what she DIDN'T do. *What if I told you that in order to get from the shy and anxious person she was, to the confident person she is today, was work on her own self-confidence and self-esteem?*

That doesn't mean she doesn't feel those exact feelings that you feel, it just means she doesn't allow them to control her. She's changed her thoughts on perfectionism; she gives herself a break, and she's altered how she feels about herself. She sees public speaking as a challenge and is willing to face her fear. She's also adopted a level of acceptance for herself and she knows that making mistakes is part of life. Even if things don't go to plan, she dusts herself off, learns from the experience and strives to do better next time. Working on herself, including her confidence and self-esteem has allowed her to become the person she is today and face her fears.

> *"To overcome fear is the quickest way to gain your self-confidence."*
>
> Roy T. Bennett, The Light in the Heart
> (Goodreads.com, 2020)[ii]

The point here is that everyone feels like you do from time to time, as we all have self-doubts or feel anxious but overcoming the fear by tackling it head on can boost confidence levels. These fearful feelings aren't unique, you just deal with them differently and by developing your self-confidence and self-esteem, you can learn to change your mindset and the way you deal with specific situations too. Our confidence and self-esteem are a projection of how we feel about ourselves so if we can start to see ourselves differently, we can better cope with the negativities that affect them.

Women have so many different roles and pressures in

their lives as we take on everything. We are daughters, wives, sisters, and mothers, but more and more women put pressure on themselves to excel in their career and education too. This is just the tip of the iceberg because women are warriors. We face every battle head on, and we are harsh on ourselves if we falter. Even if we do have confidence, we always want to do better and some of us can't shake that feeling of being an imposter – that we're just not good enough. It's because we take on so much, that we sometimes feel overwhelmed and our confidence can dip. Throughout this book, we will work on coping and self-belief strategies that will help you reframe your thoughts and change the way you think and handle situations. This will change how you see yourself.

When a person feels good about themselves it can really change how other people see them too because that confidence shines through. Many studies suggest that people who are confident and strive for success are more likely to achieve it. By working on ourselves, we can really start to focus on what we want in life and the things that make us happy. Shyness is such a common trait that it's often something that we don't consider as being a major barrier. However shyness can soon develop into anxiety too and this can damage our self-confidence.

In hindsight, shyness only becomes a barrier if we don't have the strength to overcome this. If we apply for a job and feel nervous about the interview because we don't know what we'll say, that's normal. If we don't apply because of these feelings, then this is a whole new level of shyness that can be damaging. Both the nervousness for the interview and the refusal to even apply for the job is often because the shyness has escalated and caused anxieties. Again, this impacts our levels of self-confidence.

If you would like to find your self-confidence and are ready to stop allowing your doubts, anxieties, and shyness to control your life, this book is for you. With this 30-day recovery plan you can start to work on yourself. This will lead you on a journey of self-discovery and help you build, repair and develop your confidence the right way.

It's time to change your life, and overcome those barriers, for good!

Chapter 1

Discover self-confidence and why it's worth developing

Have you ever wondered why you feel the way you do or why you doubt yourself? Often the way we judge ourselves isn't fair, because we are programmed to be hard on ourselves. We often have high expectations of ourselves, so we set goals and targets that we don't really think we can achieve. *So, why do we set them?* Basically, we set ourselves up to fail and as we don't like failure, this affects us and the way we feel about ourselves. Those feelings affect our self-confidence.

We fear failure when failure really isn't something to fear, it's something that we can embrace. You're probably thinking, *that's crazy,* but what if I told you that we can use it to help us develop and improve?

Would you like to stop being so hard on yourself and improve your self-belief? If so, you're ready to take the next step...

What is self-confidence?

Defining self-confidence isn't easy. Self-confidence is a feeling, but it's a feeling that can affect the person we are and how we think, act, or behave. It's the way we feel about ourselves and this differs from person to person. To put it simply, if you are self-confident, you believe in your own abilities, qualities, judgements and beliefs. If you aren't confident, you doubt yourself and don't believe in yourself, and this can have instrumental repercussions on what you do in your life. That means that when we do something, we question whether we did it correctly or effectively. We often assume that we won't do well, and this lack of confidence can affect our performance or our ability to handle specific situations. It can also affect how we feel, and this impacts how we live our life as we stop making changes and taking chances.

Our self-confidence influences our feelings and behavior. It can impact many things including our work life, relationships and even our family life. Those who lack confidence can face struggles with anxiety and sometimes end up doing things that they don't want to do because they are too anxious or shy to say no. They might get overlooked for that promotion because they are too afraid to speak out. They doubt their own abilities and make assumptions about themselves. For instance, they could meet the man of their dreams, but because of previous relationships failing, they believe that this relationship is doomed from the start. Due to this attitude and belief, their relationship can suffer because it's already defeated in the person's mind, so they don't accept it to succeed. In the movie, *Anger*

Management (Segal, 2003)[iii] the main character Dave was bullied as a child and particular events from his past cause him to almost lose the love of his life because he can't admit his feelings in public. Furthermore, his own fear of public embarrassment is what allows his boss to steal his design ideas. This comedy portrays how previous life events can affect the person we become. Luckily, after a series of crazy events, Dave overcomes his anxieties.

People who are confident stand out. People can rely on them because they know they will get an honest answer. They believe in themselves, and that shows in everything they do, and it encourages other people to believe in them too. Confidence brings charisma, and it's a success magnet. Theodore Roosevelt (Goodreads, 2019) once said, "Believe you can and you're halfway there."[iv] This is a true statement. If we don't believe, we allow our fear of failure to hold us back. This doesn't mean confident people never feel nervous or anxious, it just means they can cope with their feelings and they don't allow it to shape their thoughts and actions. People who lack confidence don't know how to handle those feelings and thoughts, and therefore aren't in control of their own success. This means they feel like they've failed before they begin – they accept defeat and therefore they allow themselves to be defeated easily. It's easy to become stuck in the rut of self-doubt but only those who take action to improve and work on themselves have the ability to climb out and flourish.

What is self-esteem?

Self-esteem is closely related to self-confidence, in fact it's part of it. Over the last 50 years there has been a major self-esteem movement, focusing on how it can be used to improve success, especially in children. When it comes to self-esteem, Positive Psychology claims that self-esteem is one of the basic human motivations from Maslow's hierarchy of needs and when the need is fulfilled, we grow and thrive. They suggest that there are three components that make up self-esteem.

This includes:

- It's an essential human need that ensures healthy development.
- It is automatically shaped from your personal beliefs.
- It can impact how we think, act, feel and behave (PositivePsychology.com, 2019)[v].

If someone has low self-esteem, they can be seen to have very little self-respect too. This is because they tend to make bad choices, often feel deflated or depressed and this can continue to have a negative impact in their life. People with low self-esteem can also fall into destructive relationships and many fall into this pattern over and over again. They don't feel an ounce of self-worth, they allow others to treat them badly because they feel that they deserve it. Of course, this is ridiculous!

If you have high self-esteem it can be just as destructive, so there has to be a realistic balance. It is not acceptable to live your life assuming that you're better than others or that the world owes you something; attitudes like this can ruin careers and relationships.

If we want to build and improve our self-esteem and self-confidence, we first need to work on ourselves and develop a level of self-acceptance. Only then can we achieve self-actualization, which helps us discover who we want to be and what we want in life. *So, what is that?* Well, self-actualization is having regular, powerful, valuable, and mind-blowing experiences that strengthen who we are. These experiences often mean that we have come to accept ourselves; we embrace opportunities, experiences and others, yet at the same time being realistic. When we achieve self-actualization, we are content and happy with our own company, but still, we like to have to have fun and don't feel restrained by society. They are still philosophical, autonomous and they are motivated by their values, ethics and responsibilities (Verywell Mind, 2020)[vi].

Why is self-confidence so important?

Sometimes, people have low self-confidence. This can be for numerous reasons, but it's often due to negative thought patterns that we allow to flow through our mind without question, as a result of beliefs we've formed over time. Sometimes events occur or some kind of anxiety is triggered, and this can also cause damage to our self-confidence. It's important to acknowledge these things, so that you can move forward and overcome the issues that have knocked down your confidence levels.

If your confidence levels are low, it can be really difficult to believe in yourself and get what you want out of life. It can instill a fear, and you stop believing that you can achieve your dreams and often many people with this fear settle for what they have. You may also need constant reassurance from others too, and this can affect the different relationships in your life. Others are drawn to happy, independent and confidence people who believe in themselves.

Self-confidence is so important because studies suggest that self-confident people are successful. There are many benefits of being self-confident and this can really shape our lives.

Self-confidence often means:

- Improved performance – When we are confident in ourselves and know we can do something well, we feel motivated. This often means that our performance is improved as we know we can do it and strive to be the best.

- Social ease – A confident person who is confident in their own skin is more relaxed in social situations. Their confidence and self-belief shine through in their personality and others often feel drawn to their charisma. That's because their positivity, energy and success acts as a magnet.

- Improved health – Studies suggest that good self-confidence and self-esteem indicate good mental health. That doesn't suggest that people who are confident do not have mental health issues, but just that they have the right tools to be able to cope and deal with situations that could stir up feelings of anxiety, self-doubt and shyness. It often fuels our social skills and these days, there is a lot of confidence building work in schools so that young people can adopt these tools from a young age. This can help them deal with exam and peer pressure.

- Happiness – If you feel good about yourself you are happy, and if you are happy, it can lead to you getting what you want out of life. A self-confident person isn't afraid of doing things that make them happy, as it's all part of taking care of themselves. This means that they feel in control as they recognize their own strengths and weaknesses, but while they play on their strengths, they work to develop and improve their weaknesses. Being happy and striving forward removes the fear. Fear is what prevents us from moving forward in live so with a positive attitude, you can be ready to face any obstacles head-on, because you aren't afraid to fail. You see failure as a change to learn something new or develop a skill, rather than stopping and feeling defeated.

- The ability to inspire others – Have you ever watched a person and thought, *wow, they are awesome?* They were confident and charismatic, and you felt a strong admiration. This could be a public speaker, or someone who is famous or well-known. Well that's a confident person and because their charisma and confidence shines, it inspires other people. Especially if they have a story to tell that you can relate too. We are constantly inspired by confident people, because let's face it, if someone sat quietly, was unsocial and didn't speak much, then how are you supposed to get to know them? Someone who is confident puts themselves out there and often displays a little vulnerability about their own life. Again, this inspires others and you could be a person that inspires other people if you build and develop your own self-confidence.

Small steps you can take right now to improve your self-confidence

This book will explore self-confidence, and help you develop your own over a longer period of time so that you can get what you want in life. There are some steps you can take right now to improve your confidence and self-esteem. Some of them, we will cover in more depth later, but if you want to make some small, fast changes, try these steps below:

- When you wake up in the morning, write down three things you are thankful for. It's time to do something different so if you usually sit quietly in a team meeting, barely speak to the coffee barista that serves you coffee, or you stand quietly in the playground away from the other parents, try something new. Speak! Say hello, comment about the weather, say something interesting or contribute to the team meeting and state your opinion or idea. This can make you feel happy and even proud of yourself.

- Spend some time every day on you. Taking care of yourself is important and even if it's something like reading, going for a walk, going for a coffee with your friend, or taking a long bath, it's important for your own health and happiness.

- Do something kind or help another person. Taking time away from ourselves and doing something for another can really help us to focus. Just taking some time to focus on something can help us to move away from our negative thinking patterns.

- Walk away, breathe and take a few moments to collect your thoughts. Sometimes we can be a little irrational when we aren't feeling confident as those feelings of anxiousness become too much. Sometimes a brisk walk, a chat with a friend or just some air can make a wealth of difference.

Start your 30-day Recovery Plan Activities

It's important to start making progress with your

confidence now, to see maximum results. That's why we've devised some steps for you each day for the next 30 days, so that you can start to work on yourself and slowly make changes and explore your confidence, then you can figure out what you want from life and what makes you happy.

Journaling is a huge part of this workbook as it has endless benefits, and it is suggested that you embrace this concept for the whole of the 30-days at least. Journaling has so many benefits because it can help you to feel calm, encourage you to solve issues and problems, it helps you make sense of your thoughts and actions, while gaining clarity, and it can also increase your creativity. Throughout this book we reflect on negative thought patterns and actions, so journaling will help you to track and monitor those patterns too. A key benefit of journaling is that it helps you get those thoughts out of your head and on paper. Many people report that if they journal in the evening before bed, they sleep better. That's because you are putting your thoughts and ideas on paper, so you don't have them swimming around your head all night. This way, you don't need to worry in case you forget them.

If you've never journaled before, don't worry. This guide will help you through each three-day cycle and provide prompts and ideas to help you journal with ease. Soon, it will become second nature!

Day 1-3 of your 30-day Recovery Plan

You may have heard of journaling before and it's a great way to start organizing your thoughts as it helps you to identify any problems and anything that holds you back.

START YOUR JOURNAL
Your first task is to start a journal and write in it for three days of your self-confidence journey. You can use the prompts below to reflect on what we've covered in chapter 1 if you aren't sure of what to write:
- What aspects of your self-esteem and self-confidence hold you back?
- Did any of the traits highlighted in the chapter resonate with you? Write them out.

- Write a description or profile of the person you aspire to be – think about what you would do if you weren't holding yourself back.
- How does it make you feel when your confidence is lacking?
- Are there any patterns in the way you think or act? Is this a new feeling or have you always felt like that? Are there any events that trigger how you feel?

Practice journaling in a style that suits you over the next 3 days.

ACTIONABLE STEP

Examine your journal after the first three days and see if you can see any patterns in the way you think or act. We all behave in a certain way, so this is normal.

Do something different to disrupt this pattern. For example, if you don't speak out at work or in meetings, try it. This is often empowering. *How did you feel after you disrupted the pattern?*

ACTIVITY

When we first start analyzing our behavior and thought patterns, they can be overwhelming. We might not know why we react in a particular way or why we aren't confident. Calming the mind is really important to this whole process.

If you start to feel overwhelmed, try this activity to calm you down. Earlier in this chapter, we talked about walking away and taking some time.

Relaxed breathing can really help with this:

- Take yourself off to somewhere quiet.
- Sit down, relax, and close your eyes.
- Breathe in for five seconds and out for seven.
- Try to clear your mind by concentrating on the rhythm.
- Repeat the words "I am worthy of taking up space" 3 times.
- Absorb the feeling of confidence for another 10 seconds.

Open your eyes and go back to whatever you were doing before.

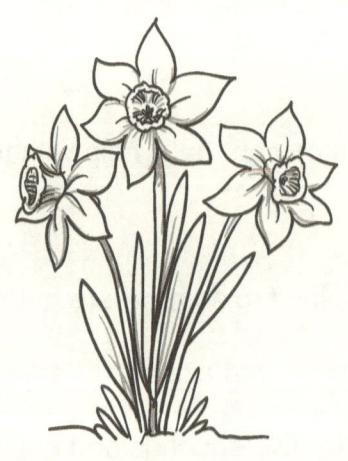

Chapter 2

Observe Your Present Self to Move Forward without Judgment

It's said that we are our own biggest critic and it's true that we are often harsh on ourselves. We often don't consider using our critiquing abilities for the greater good, but when it comes to our confidence, this is certainly possible. You see, critiquing is in fact a skill, and there's a rule you must observe when critiquing your confidence levels… in order to critique effectively, you need to back up your findings with an observation or evidence.

If you're going to make judgments, you should be sure to justify it. Negative judgments can appear nasty, so it's important to communicate them in an effective and constructive way and always think of something positive to say!

Observing your current state of confidence

A person with low confidence often behaves in specific ways that gives us a clue about their current confidence level. Use the quiz below to assess your current state of confidence:

1. How easy do you make decisions? Are you…?
    a) *Indecisive. I never know if I'm making the right decision and I can never decide whether I should or shouldn't do something.*
    b) *Sometimes indecisive but other times I know what I want.* It depends on the situation as sometimes I know exactly what I want and other times I don't.
    c) *I know what I want and make decisions with ease.*

There is no self-doubt, you just make your decision and go for it.

2. If I have to speak in front of others or explain anything, I feel…
   a) *Flustered, and a little scared.* I dread these situations and worry about them for days.
   b) *Unsure.* I can usually put my worries in the back of my mind and focus on what I need to do. I still worry but I get on with it.
   c) *Excited.* I thrive in situations like this. I enjoy speaking in front of others.

3. How easily do you confront others?
   a) I don't, I avoid it. I only do this if absolutely necessary, but it provokes emotion.
   b) *I do it in the nicest way possible, often apologizing beforehand and after.*
   c) *I put my professional head on, plan what I should say, and speak confidently about the matter.*

4. If I fail, I…
   a) *Give up.* I knew it was going to fail, it's my own fault.

b) *Think, "at least I tried". I talk it through with someone and eventually I might try again.*

c) *Consider the experience a learning curve. I analyze where I went wrong, ask advice from others, and I try again.*

5. You are asked to do something difficult that you've never done before. You say...
   a) *I can't.*
   b) *I'll give it a go.*
   c) *I'll do it.* Then you ask lots of questions.

Mostly A:

You need to work on your confidence issues as they are currently holding you back. You are in danger of self-doubt controlling everything you do, but now it's time to start moving forward. Everyone around you knows that great things are ahead of you, but you currently don't see your own worth. You need to believe in yourself and increase your confidence as eventually, people could stop reminding you. You're the master of your own destiny – write a list of everything you know, and I mean EVERYTHING. You might even surprise yourself!

Mostly B:

You have some confidence issues and although they hold you back, they aren't too overwhelming at this time. You do try to make a stand and control your self-doubt, but you haven't mastered this yet. You are in danger of allowing confidence issues to escalate, so it's really important that you keep developing your confidence. Take some time to clear your mind and relax, so you can start to see what you really want in life. Set some goals for yourself and start pushing – if you really want something, you need to grab it with both hands. Keep building, growing and learning – don't back down or give up because what you want is within reach.

Mostly C:

Your confidence levels are good, and you have a good attitude that will help you grow and develop. Just be careful that you maintain those confidence levels as they will help you get what you really want in life. There are some great ways you can work on maintaining your confidence and even though you're doing well, don't stop setting goals and striving for more. It's important that you schedule in some time for yourself too, to ensure you're heading for what you really want. Don't be afraid to reassess what you want and if you change your mind, that's fine – we're allowed to change our course. Ensure you aren't too hard on yourself too, as this can be damaging to your confidence. Reach for the stars, we know you've got this!

You've done the quiz, so you know what level your confidence is at presently – but what other signs indicate that you have low self-esteem? Many people don't even notice when their confidence is slipping, so here are some common signs.

9 Common Signs that your confidence is dipping

When your confidence is starting slip, it's hard to initially recognize the signs. One minute, everything is going fine, and before you know it things have spiraled out of control. We can prevent this spiral if we are aware of some of the signs. A dip in confidence can start with a feeling of unease, or anxiousness, at a gradual rate.

These feelings can stem from feeling nervous about something and they creep up on you.

The 9 most common signs are:
- Backing down in a disagreement, just because it's easier and it avoids conflict. We can do this even if we are right, but we can't face a draining argument, or we're worried that we don't get our point across effectively.
- If someone makes a constructive comment to help you, you find yourself emotional or upset; you see these things as a personal attack, even though your rational mind knows they are not.
- You like to have your make-up done or hair done and can't answer the door or leave the home if you're not at a specific standard.
- When you're in a social situation, you'd rather check your phone every couple of minutes than talk to others.
- When someone pays you a compliment, you shy away because you don't know how to react.
- It's difficult for you to make decisions, even simple ones. You change your mind constantly.

- You don't like to voice your own opinion because you're afraid that anything you say would not be valid.
- You tend to self-sabotage your own chances, because you always feel unworthy and feel like another person (often anyone) is more suitable for a specific task than you are. You compare yourself to them and think of reasons why you shouldn't do things.
- When you don't succeed on your first attempt, you stop or give up because you feel like you're not going to be successful anyway, so you should quit sooner rather than later (Lifehack, 2020)[vii].

Making Judgments

We've talked a lot about being naturally hard on ourselves and it's time to think a little more about that. We can sometimes make judgments or assumptions based on our own beliefs or also depending on how we feel, but it's important to refrain from making judgments when exploring confidence. Making judgments and assumptions can be toxic. If your confidence is low already and you start shooting yourself down further, it could lead to further issues, like depression, and you may even give up or stop working on your confidence. Confidence is complex and it's closely linked to self-belief, self-esteem, self-worth, as well as anxiety and other mental health conditions. It is often a tiny piece of a thousand-piece puzzle, but without it, you are not complete. Improving our confidence can be the final piece when improving our mind, body and spirit, but until we understand its make-up, and how we can develop or improve it, we should never make judgments regarding others or ourselves because issues could be embedded much deeper. Judgments and assumptions are often the root of the demise of confidence, so bear that in mind as you continue exploring yours.

Judgments are often the foundations we use for decision-making and while it's important not to dwell on the judgments of others, you still need to make judgments in your own life. In order to make a justified judgement, you need to pay attention to both sides – the positives and negatives. You should also be aware of the impact your judgment will have – *would somebody lose their job because you made a judgment about their work ethics?* It's important that you take an outside perspective and listen to the views of others. Ensure you know your topic and receive any advice or guidance as needed – there's never any harm in asking others to help or contribute.

By making judgments, we become accountable for actions or decisions. Taking responsibility is a massive step if confidence is low, so don't be afraid to ask for support if needed.

Does my self-esteem stem from my childhood?

Many people question whether their self-esteem issues are embedded from childhood, and this is a good, yet complex question. We do carry many beliefs from our childhood, and it can be difficult to change them into something positive. If we were made to feel inadequate as a child, then this feeling of worthlessness can hold us back in the future. It can mean we don't take certain opportunities throughout our lives because we don't want to be embarrassed or made to feel unworthy again.

It is suggested that children have high self-esteem and low self-esteem can be related to physical punishment or a lack of affection or love from their family. That does not mean that this is the only reason. A child who is generally unhappy or is bullied
can have low self-esteem too and it can also result in in them treating others unfairly too. Children with low self-esteem can withdraw themselves and often struggle socially, which can also become a problem in adulthood. They often do not have fun and lack confidence in fear of being ridiculed. As they fear failure, they quit things easily, cheat, avoid situations they don't like and some even turn into bullies as they adopt negative coping strategies.

In teenagers, self-esteem can also dip and sometimes this is in relation to puberty and body image. Obviously, when teenagers start to experience feelings due to hormone changes, they have to learn to cope with these and it can take some time to control feelings and emotions. As their bodies change, they can also start to consider pictures in magazines as being the ideal and if they feel they need to look like that, it can make them feel low about themselves. Teenagers are vulnerable and influenced easily. If they struggle to feel good enough or comfortable with themselves and their own body, it can cause their self-esteem to plummet.

Inevitably, if you did not deal with these issues as a child, then you will take them with you into adulthood. The longer you believe the beliefs ingrained into you as a child, the more difficult it is to change them. But it's not impossible! (Mcleod, 2012)[viii].

The Psychology of Self-Confidence

It's obvious that some people struggle with self-confidence while others don't, *but why is that?* In truth, self-confidence is a personal, individual thing, because it's the way we view ourselves and it has a lot to do with how we personally feel. Many things can contribute to how we feel or view ourselves. Our genes, culture, and all other circumstances that we live through, such as bullying, abuse (mental and physical), and trauma can influence our self-confidence. It's whether we can work through them and make the difference, that matters.

Many studies suggest that some self-confidence traits are programmed in us since birth. They have focused on genetics and how the chemicals in our brain make a difference to self-confidence. We can have different serotonin (which is said to stimulate happiness) and oxytocin (the cuddle hormone) levels, which can mean we adopt different personality traits and it's those that impact whether or not confidence is inherited. Obviously, those with higher self-esteem levels produce those happy hormones in the brain (Psychology Today, 2018)[ix]. There are many studies that highlight the neuroscience behind this idea as they suggest that people who demonstrate several low self-esteem traits, suffer more social pain from social exclusion. People who demonstrate higher levels of self-esteem, suffer less social pain from social exclusion (Onoda et al.,

2010)[x]. This is because they are generally happier and have stronger coping mechanisms to deal with any exclusions.

Sometimes we don't understand the rules of self-confidence because we've never been taught them and often this is because our heads have been filled with the wrong information. For example, if we were brought up to think that only being perfect is acceptable, it can cause a major impact on our lives. In truth, nobody is perfect! Often, other things can affect our self-confidence too, and it's often that feeling of not fitting in, which could be down to things like gender, age, sexual orientation and race. If you've ever been discriminated against or humiliated, it can become increasingly difficult to feel comfortable with yourself as you struggle to belong. The world itself is also to blame, as everyone struggles with self-doubt now and then, and often messages portrayed in the media can make us feel inadequate too. Let's not forget that self-confidence issues can also be linked to depression and anxiety too (Psychology Today, 2018)[xi].

All these feelings and beliefs influence the way we perceive the world, and the way we think it perceives us. This all contributes to the way we view ourselves and this impacts our self-confidence. Self-confidence is complex, so it's not easy to understand. Our mind is programmed to think for itself based on our beliefs that shape it. If we can start to understand where our self-confidence issues stem from, we can certainly try to develop and improve this. Increasing self-confidence could change the way you view life and yourself, which could mean you improve your mental health and change your negative beliefs. This can ultimately enrich your life, career and relationships in the longer term.

What different behaviors suggest low self-esteem?

Low confidence and self-esteem can certainly trigger certain emotions or behaviors. We've talked about the signs of low-confidence earlier in this book, but we've been reflecting on what indicates low self-esteem in this chapter. There are some behavioral signs that can suggest you are lacking self-esteem. Below we're going to take a quick look at these behaviors and make some suggestions of how we can alter these to improve confidence and self-esteem. We have mentioned some of these already, but it's time to address and dig deep in their meaning.

Avoidance behaviors certainly signal low self-esteem. This includes quitting, avoiding situations or people, and even procrastinating or struggling to concentrate can all indicate this. This is because these behavior types stem from your fear of failure, which is part of your belief system. Since we don't like to fail, we would rather not try. Avoiding situations, people or events, means you protect yourself, as you don't want to suffer with those negative thoughts and feelings that you feel when you think you've failed (Counselling-directory.org.uk, 2016)[xii].

So, what can we possibly do to change this? Well, we need to change how you feel about failure. You see, many people view failure as a learning curve. I want you to think about when we are babies and we learn to walk. Walking takes practice, but we don't give up, we keep going until we can do it. Or talking. It takes years of practice to perfect our speech capabilities, but we don't simply stop trying. If we had this attitude about failure all of our life, we would never learn anything. To want to learn is a good thing, it's how we grow and develop. Next time, if you want to avoid a situation, think, *what you can do to make that more comfortable? What do you need to do or learn? Can you make a plan and some actionable steps of how you can face this fear?*

Perfectionist behaviors can also signal low self-esteem. If you work hard in an excessive way, you like to control everything, you're extremely competitive, like to try and please others, and act angry if things don't go your way, then you are showing perfectionist behaviors. If someone is a perfectionist, they feel that only being perfect is acceptable, and they believe they will only feel better about themselves if they meet the perfect category. They often make this impossible though, by setting goals that are unrealistic, thereby in reality, a perfectionist sets themself up for failure. This is a huge problem, because they then feel frustrated and useless (Counselling-directory.org.uk, 2016)[xiii].

In truth, nothing is perfect, and everyone makes mistakes. Ideas of perfectionism are often false. Now, it's important to still aim big, but try this strategy to change your viewpoint of perfectionism, next time when you're completing a task.

- Think about what you want to achieve – what's your best target?
- Now work backwards. What would be the worst thing that could ever happen in relation to this task? What would be disastrous?
- Think about your next target which is a step down from best. What would be a good target?
- Finally, think about your next target down from 'good'. What would be an okay target for you? What could you live with?

Now the idea here is to aim for the best but you should also accept the good and okay targets as well as think about what you could've done to improve those. How could you reach your best target? What improvements can you make to do better next time? It's very rare that the worst-case scenario will happen, so be thankful for that. If it does, it's important that again you assess why it happened and what you can change to make sure it doesn't happen again. If you constantly assess, and think about what you can do to improve, it changes your whole perspective on how you view perfectionism.

Hiding is another type of behavior that indicates low self-esteem. Now this doesn't mean hiding as in the same essence of hide and seek but hiding your real self. For example, you hide your beliefs, sexual orientation, appearance, your likes or dislikes or even religion, weaknesses and certain characteristics about yourself. It's important to consider why we feel the need to hide ourselves. For instance, if you avoid telling your family that you no longer want to be a doctor and have changed your college major because you don't want to upset them, you are hiding your true self from them. You do this to avoid conflict, to help you fit in, to prevent negative criticism or simply to please others. However, pretending to be someone else damages your own self-esteem and confidence because you are suppressing yourself (Counselling-directory.org.uk, 2016)[xiv].

A person who has higher levels of confidence copes with the idea of judgement or disappointing others in a different way, because they accept that they can't hide who they are. It can be difficult to change this belief because we can never determine how the world will respond to us and there are some judgmental people out there.

Remember that if you hide yourself for acceptance or to please others, then it stems from a deep-rooted fear that others will be disappointed in you or not accept you. A confident person is happy and comfortable with who they are, so what other people think may of course be important but it's not everything. If you aren't true to yourself and others, you're being fake and lying to yourself. This means it's impossible for you to be happy.

To deal with this, write down some beliefs that others think or have of you, then write down the truth. Write down the best thing that would happen and the worst-case scenario and assess them. *Is the worst really that bad?* If you fear people falling out with you, that could be a short-term thing while they get over the initial shock of what you've been hiding. Others may respond a lot better than you think because people are increasingly acceptant of others and want you to be, or do, whatever makes you happy. Whatever you think the worst case is, it probably wouldn't last forever, but neither will your hiding – the truth comes out eventually. Many people respect you for telling the truth. You need to really stress to yourself that your happiness comes first (within reason of course), and the important people will accept it. Facing the judgments, or disappointments felt by others is better than living a lie.

Passive behaviors are when you just can't say no, even when you don't want to do something or can't fit it in. Saying no is hard, and you may find that you dismiss your own needs and thoughts, avoid expressing your opinion, and put yourself down regularly because you doubt your own abilities and judgments (Counselling-directory.org.uk, 2016)[xv].

We can all be passive and again, this is because we don't like to disappoint others. If we constantly say yes and do things that we don't want to or can't do, it can really affect us. Self-esteem means demonstrating the strong side of yourself, so in order to do that, you need to say no from time to time. If passive behavior is one of your traits, write down three occasions when you've said yes, when you really needed to say no, and think about how this affected you.

Write down how you would've liked to respond but ensure it's in a positive way as we don't need to get held back by the negative. Also, don't apologize! It's easy for someone to start saying things like *'I'm sorry, but I can't...'*

Why are you sorry?

Remember, you have a right to your own thoughts and feelings so own them. Speak your mind and don't doubt yourself.

Write down a list of phrases you can use to turn someone down next time they ask you to do something you just can't or don't want to do. Planning ahead is key here because you are no longer put on the spot and feel obliged to say yes. Saying no shows strength and confidence – you've got this!

Attention-seeking behaviors Sometimes when people suffer with low self-esteem or confidence, they behave in a way that grabs the attention of others. For example, they may behave in ways that are risky or dangerous, try to get sympathy from others, seek compliments from others, request reassurances from others that they are doing the right thing, or they may believe they aren't capable of doing certain things so they ask someone else to do it for them. A lot of these may come from the belief that they are not good enough, others are better, or they may need constant reassurances to make themselves feel better (Counselling-directory.org.uk, 2016)[xvi].

To avoid attention seeking behavior, you really need to assess yourself and write a list of the attention seeking behaviors you show. Next time you find yourself seeking compliments or reassurances from others, stop and give yourself one. Think about why you behave in a particular way and write some affirmations about believing in your self – you don't need others to react (in a positive or negative way), so focus on self-belief, rather than the beliefs of others. If you react in a risky or dangerous way, then you may need to get some help to work through your problems. Don't be afraid to get some help if you need it!

Aggressive behavior is another sign. Sometimes people with low confidence or self-esteem can react in an aggressive way as they try to fill in the gap, where their self worth and self-esteem is missing. Acting aggressively can be putting people down, shouting, and demanding things, and they can often blame others for the negative thoughts or feelings they have.

While jealousy to a certain level can be healthy, because it means you want to strive to have more for yourself, being jealous of others can also be toxic and can indicate a low level of self-esteem. A person with low self-esteem can struggle with developmental feedback or criticism too because they take it negatively, rather than regarding it as a learning experience or something to develop. Self-confidence and self-esteem have a lot to do with how we view and feel about ourselves (Counselling-directory.org.uk, 2016)[xvii].

Aggressive behavior isn't a great trait to suffer from because it can certainly hold you back as it portrays you in a negative light. Keep a diary of any aggressive behavior to monitor this and write down how you feel. Sometimes people just need to be aware of their aggressive behavior and they can come up with techniques to deal with it. Breathing exercises are a great way to calm yourself and clear your mind, but if you find that you feel a lot of anger and resentment, don't be afraid to seek professional medical help as there could be an underlying issue that is driving your low confidence and self-esteem. People under stress or depression can certainly act out, so keep a diary, try some breathing techniques and monitor how you feel. Seek medical help if it's out of control.

If some of the behaviors above link to how you react, this means you are starting to grow an awareness of how your low self-esteem and confidence is affecting you. When you're aware, you can start to monitor this and once you can monitor, you can improve and challenge those thoughts and behaviors.

How quickly can I improve my self-esteem?

There is no simple answer to this question. Self-esteem can be something that we need to work on regularly, if not constantly. While there are some quick fixes to self-esteem as soon as you become aware of the signaling behaviors, it may take a lot more time to get to the root of the problem.

If you read the list of behaviors in the previous section, and you relate to many of them, it can become overwhelming. With that in mind, you need to remember one key point – *every small change or step is progress.* It's a good idea to start changing your behaviors slowly, one at a time, and cement your new way of thinking before you move onto the next. This is suggested to be a healthier way as you are less likely to fail. To work on yourself at a slow pace requires patience, and for someone with low self-esteem, this isn't as simple as it sounds. You deserve the time, effort and dedication so stay motivated.

This leads to my next question, *what motivates you to succeed?* There must be something and this something might be the key to succeeding when it comes to increasing your self-esteem.

Days 4-6 of your 30-day Recovery Plan

JOURNALING

How's your journaling going? Journaling should be part of your daily routine but if you're struggling, start to think about what we've covered in chapter 2 in relation to self-esteem and the behaviors we display.

PROMPT: *Is there anything I did today that caused a reaction, that I would do differently?*

*Highlight behavior episodes that indicate your low

self-esteem. Use a highlighter or different colored pen to make them stand out (just put a small squiggle or star close to your notes), so you can spot them easily.

ACTIONABLE STEP

Review your journal and choose two or three reactions/behaviors to analyze. Start by putting them into a table:

- What behavior did you exhibit?
- What triggered this/what happened?
- How did you feel/react?
- How do you feel you should've reacted?
- What would be the best/worst possible outcome?
- How can you change this behavior/response or what would you do differently next time?

ACTIVITY – Plan to change

Look at your behaviors and look for patterns – are any behaviors similar to the different types discussed in chapter 2 (hiding, aggressive, passive etc...)?

Choose one behavior type that you feel holds you back

the most or is the most destructive and focus on that one. *For example, if you exhibit hiding behaviors, list the hiding behaviors that you've shown over the last few days. This could be holding you back because you feel anxious.*

Think about the types of situations that attract this behavior from you and plan a new response. Maybe you've hidden one of your skills at work or are hiding the fact you're completing a degree, in case people judge you or embarrass you, or ask you something you don't know. *Write how you do respond and write out how you want to respond.*

Finally, write out the best and worst outcome of this. For example, people could congratulate you and wish you well (best). Someone tells you degrees are a waste of time, they never needed one (worst), or goes on a rant about degrees being a waste of money. Regardless – does that really matter? Assess the worst outcome with the best. *Is the worst that bad? How will you respond?* Planning in advance is key to your success, so you aren't put on the spot.

Plan to make a small behavior change and when you achieve it, be proud – journal about it and how it made you feel!

Chapter 3

Tackle Shyness to Present Your Authenticity in Any Crowd

Do you ever want to hide, or maybe you want the ground to open up and swallow you? At least that would get you away from the situation you've found yourself in, *right?*

Well that's all fine but sadly, hiding will never solve your shyness issues...

It's common to be shy, especially when meeting new people, but shyness can really hold us back. Shyness sometimes means we don't introduce ourselves to others, so it can affect us on a social level. It can impact our job interviews, relationships, the way we work, and it can make us feel anxious. If we are shy, we tend to melt into the background of everything and we try not to draw attention to ourselves. When we do, it's extremely embarrassing! The problem is this shyness holds us back and stops us from getting the best out of ourselves. *But what is exactly is shyness and how can we overcome this for good?*

What is shyness, how it develops and ways to move past it?

Shyness is a part of our personality, in fact it's a personality trait. People who are shy, do not introduce themselves or communicate as quickly or as confidently as someone who is not shy or is confident. This is because they hesitate. They may have anxiety or they could worry: *Will I say the right thing?* Or *what should I say?* And they often just need that little extra time to think and gather themselves.

Shyness is a normal part of our personality, but the level of shyness can depend on our personal temperament. Sometimes people are extremely shy, and this can develop further by escalating stress and anxiety levels that can cause extreme anxiety. It can then grow into a social anxiety disorder if we don't work on this.

If you enter a room and you don't introduce yourself right away, it becomes harder and harder to make that initial introduction. Maybe you pull out your phone, pretend you're reading, or on your phone, and maybe you slip out of social gatherings as early as possible. Imagine this… you go to a networking meeting for your organization and you constantly check your phone, you put your head down, avoid talking to others, and you say very little. You can feel yourself going red and you slip out the back way. *Was it worth going?* Not really! It would be a waste of time and completely unproductive because you didn't make that initial introduction and became so anxious that you couldn't introduce yourself at all. It got harder the longer it went on until you left.

The more we allow ourselves to be shy, the more we allow it to fester, the more overwhelmed we feel and the harder it is to overcome. One of the ways to overcome shyness is to face to situations that make us feel shy, but on a controlled level. The idea is that you should take things slowly and not give up but celebrate the small wins along the way. Once we make progress and our confidence grows, our shyness will become easier to control.

What's the difference between shyness and introversion?

There are a lot of links made between introversion and shyness. This is because both can influence the way we communicate with others or the actions we take. If you're shy or an introvert, then you probably aren't as social as others. Some studies suggest that a key difference is that people who are shy, don't choose to feel as socially awkward when it comes to communicating with others, while an introvert has a choice. Someone who is shy may find it really difficult to communicate with others and this can actually start to make them feel anxious. An introvert doesn't get anxious when it comes to interacting with others, but they just don't particularly like or want to interact or communicate (Curtin, 2018)[xviii].

While shyness can be linked to anxiety and you do become introverted, the two are very different. Sometimes people are not sure whether they are shy, an introvert or an extrovert, but this is a very good question… We already know that to be shy, you feel anxious about social and communicative situations, and you can't control how you feel.

According to *Introvert Dear (2019)*, you're more of an introvert if you like being alone and having time for inner reflection, if socializing drains you both mentally and physically, if you enjoy writing and often prefer thinking to talking. An introvert often prefers to have deep relationships, so long-term friends or partners are common, rather than casual ones. Although an introvert is an excellent listener, they expect this in return and tend to look at life from the inside out. *Does this sound more like you?*

If you're more of an extrovert, then you get your energy from others and thrive on the social aspects in life as being alone brings you down. An extrovert is also interested in the world and is more of a talker rather than a listening – they think at their best when they are speaking. Extroverts often convey themselves in a more confident way as they can express themselves well, verbally, they are friendly and assertive, and they always keep themselves busy. *Does this sound more like you?* (Introvert, Dear, 2019)[xix].

There are no right or wrong answers here as often, people are a combination of the two, while others lean more towards one or the other. This is part of who you are, and many things can influence this including your energy, life, work and upbringing. Your beliefs, experiences and general view of the world can also shape our personality and temperament. *So, why do we need to know this?* In truth, it isn't essential but knowing our personality and temperaments can help us to understand who we are and how we can change. If we understand why we do something, or why we behave in a particular way, it becomes easier to make sense of everything, identify anything negative, and make that change.

Social anxiety and shyness

Social anxiety is another condition associated with shyness. Shyness can trigger feelings of anxiety due to the way a person feels about a social situation. We've already discussed shyness and how it is a personality trait; it's part of who we are, but social anxiety is very different.

Social anxiety is a severe anxiety disorder that prevents a person from partaking in certain activities and situations, because they can't control their levels of anxiety. This means they avoid even some of the most regular activities. A person who suffers from this disorder have a significant amount of fear. They feel embarrassed or humiliated when it comes to social based situation, especially if they feel that they will be expected or even pressurized to take part. When a person suffers severely from this it increases stress and distress levels, which means the person would much rather avoid the situation than feel this level of fear.

Like shyness, social anxiety disorder isn't a choice but there are things we can change or adopt to improve its impact. If you suffer from either, there are coping techniques you can use to ease the feelings of anxiousness, such as the breathing exercises we started looking at in chapter 1.

Staying Authentic

It's important to remember that when changing your personality, you're in danger of changing who you are. For some, this may seem to be good thing, but for others, they may not want to change too much – quite right! You may need to change certain aspects of yourself, providing you are changing for the right reasons, but it's important to stay true to who you are.

When you start to make changes it's important that you don't try to mold your personality to suit others. If we try to be something we're not it will make us unhappy which will cause further anxiety.

When others see you, they will see a sincere person when you are being yourself, but when you try to be something or someone you're not, you will find that people are not so easily fooled. It's in our nature to see through people and we are naturally drawn to authentic and honest people who we can relate to.

Be careful not to force any changes and only change aspects of yourself. If you are not true to yourself, cracks will appear and then others will struggle to trust you. We have to accept that although we can make improvements and slight changes, we can only be ourselves. However, this is something that many people with low-confidence struggle with. This is because they feel like they are not good enough.

If you are shy or anxious, then it is part of your personality trait. If you suddenly stop being shy, people will wonder why. That's because we don't just transition from being a quiet little mouse in the corner who daren't speak, into a loudmouth, overnight. Most people will never transition in such a drastic way, nor would anyone believe it because it's too unbelievable. Whilst it's great to make personal leaps in our personal development, ensure that you are still the person you are and want to be. To do this, you should:

- Visualize your ideal self and keep working towards it.
- Make the changes you need to make, for yourself.
- Don't make the changes you feel you should make, or that other people tell you to make.
- Think about your core beliefs in life and follow them. Don't stray!

With all of the conditions we've compared in this chapter, it is clear that there are similarities between social anxiety, shyness, and introversion. They can have similar traits as we've discovered but they are all very different too. So, *how do we take action to improve our confidence when there's so many things to overcome?*

There are a variety of techniques that we will unravel throughout this book and as every person is different, it's a case of trying them and seeing which works best for you.

If you suffer from shyness and social anxiety, you need to focus on changing your negative thinking patterns and you should also set yourself little challenges, so you can make progress. For example, you can use affirmations and goal setting to help yourself overcome your barriers. Your goals should be focused around engagement and trying new things. You can also use breathing strategies to learn how to cope in uncomfortable situations too. Obviously, it depends on the levels of your shyness and social anxieties, but make sure you celebrate any wins, no matter how small they are. Don't be afraid to get help and advice from professionals if you need it.

When it comes to introversion, you can use similar techniques, like goal setting and trying new things. If you are simply an introvert, it's likely that you won't need to do the coping techniques because if you are an introvert, this is usually a choice or preference. Again, make sure you celebrate your wins. As an introvert, it is likely that you don't like to draw attention to yourself but think about the type of person you would like to be and use small goals to make those personality changes. It is likely that you'll have to work on your own beliefs and attitude to help you take a different view and react differently to social situations. If you keep practicing social interactions and setting small goals, you will soon overcome this barrier as it will become second nature in the future.

Day 7-9 of your 30-day Recovery Plan

CONTINUE JOURNALING – Day 7-9
How is your journaling going? You're a week in now, so journaling should be part of your routine now. Make sure that journaling logs both your positive and negative experiences from the week.

*Spend some time reflecting on your first week of journaling. *Did you manage to change or disrupt one of* *your behavior patterns?*

ACTIONABLE STEP

During days 7-9, you're going to take some small steps to discovering your ideal self. Follow the steps for each day, below:

- Day 7 – Describe the personality of your ideal self. Are they confident? Happy? What do they like? How do they handle uncomfortable situations?
- Day 8 – Reflect on your ideal self. Think about you now. What do you need to do to transform into that ideal person? Set yourself 3-5 goals here.
- Day 9 – Spend some time reflecting on the last 8 days and keep your ideal self in mind. Think about difficulties you've faced and identify how you handled this. *Would you do anything different? How did you react? How should you react?* If you reacted well, be proud! Ask yourself, *how would the ideal me respond to this, what would they do?* Don't just look at the bad situations, look at the good too!

ACTIVITY

We've talked about our ideal self but think about who you are now.

Consider the points below:

- *What do you really want or need?*
- Are you shy, an introvert, or socially anxious?
- *Imagine yourself in an awkward situation that you usually avoid. Write a list of how you feel and how you would react in this situation.*
- *Make a list of three things you would like to change in your life.* This can be to do with jobs and careers, having more family or personal time, self-care, anything personal, material items, relationships.

Analyze your list and consider if any of these display traits of being an introvert, being shy, or socially anxious. Think about how your traits hold you back and really think about how you can overcome any barriers.

Keep hold of your list as it's an important part of your recovery!

Chapter 4

Move from Self-Doubt into Self-Trust to Solidify Your Internal Relationship

"The moment you doubt whether you can fly, you cease for ever to be able to do it."

J. M. Barrie, Peter Pan (Goodreads.com, 2020)[xx]

We all feel self-doubt from time-to-time, but have you thought about the impact this can have if it escalates?

As soon as we doubt ourselves, the trouble begins. As *J. M. Barrie* says above, as soon as we doubt, we may never be able to undo it. Now while that sentiment isn't wholly true, it is harder to fix feelings of self-doubt once they've occurred. Feelings of self-doubt can quite easily spiral out of control and once we've had them, the more difficult it becomes to remove them from our mind. This is all connected to the relationship we have with ourselves. Self-doubt is an internal barrier that some people feel daily and it prevents us from moving forward. After all, if you don't have trust in yourself or you doubt your own capabilities, *how can you expect anyone else to believe in you?*

Where does self-doubt come from?

It's human nature to question ourselves and our own abilities. We always wonder if we're good enough or qualified enough, and we often believe there is someone out there who is better than us. We put ourselves down and we believe these knee-jerk reactions and thoughts. Human nature makes us sell ourselves short but really, to be a specialist in a particular area, we just need to know more than the other people we're working with or speaking to. For instance, if you attend a meeting about the rainforest, the guest speaker would know more about the rain forest and the problems it faces than you do. They may not know everything, but we would count them as being an expert in that area. Even though that's how we view others, a lot of people struggle to see themselves as an expert in their field. Even if you don't know it yet, there will be something that you are a specialist or expert in!

Self-doubt ultimately comes from the relationship we have with ourselves. Think about how many times you question your actions and feelings… You probably can't remember the exact number of times you question yourself, but this can increase over time and it can set in feelings of panic. One way to monitor self-doubt is to note the event and what happened down in your journal.

Self-doubt is all about the way we view our own worth and how harsh we are with ourselves. Even the most qualified and experienced person in the world can feel uncomfortable in their own skin and often feel like an imposter. You might have heard of imposter syndrome before...

Where does imposter syndrome come from?

Imposter syndrome is an internalized fear. This term is often used in psychology to describe a lack of self-belief in ourselves and our own achievements. Many famous people and instrumental figures have admitted to suffering from imposter syndrome. It's more common than you think, but up until recently, people didn't really admit to this. This is because they were afraid to own up to this fear publicly because nobody likes to show weakness.

The admission of major public figures suffering with imposter syndrome recently has really brought to light just how common it is. Michelle Obama admitting this was surprising for many people – *How on earth can a former First Lady feel like she's an imposter?* But the truth is, anyone can feel like this. When speaking at a school, Michelle was told she was seen as 'a beacon of hope' and she admitted that her imposter syndrome never goes away, and she sometimes can't believe that people are really there to listen to her (Impostor Syndrome, 2020)[xxi].

There are now different perspectives on this, because showing a vulnerability keeps us human and it shows that no matter who we are: movie stars, entrepreneurs, public figures, sports stars, or political marvels, showing a little vulnerability grounds them. They are people, just like us and we share this trait. The fact that they can speak about this motivates us and gives us hope – if they can do it, so can we!

Imposter syndrome often comes from our core beliefs. Look at the statements below:
- *I've never been one of the popular kids.*
- *People who live in my neighborhood never make millions.*
- *Nobody in my family has ever studied in higher education.*

If you are brought up to believe any of the statements above or something similar, the likelihood is, you will believe this for most of your life... unless you take action to change these beliefs.

While some people suggest that imposter syndrome is a personality or character trait of a person, it can hold you back and it can bring on anxiety issues because imposter syndrome instils fear. Sometimes despite our experience and qualifications in life, we just don't feel good enough and we fear being exposed as a fraud. While this isn't a disorder, it is an internal belief in which people believe they do not deserve success. They simply categorize their successes as being good luck or being in the right place at the right time, rather than realizing and acknowledging their competence (Dalla-Camina, 2018)[xxii].

What are self-limiting beliefs and how do we overcome them?

Overcoming something that's embedded in our mind

and soul is never easy but when something is holding you back, you have to start to think about 'why'. Self-limiting beliefs are when we assume or believe something, and it prevents us or limits us from doing something else or moving on with our life. This is a tricky thing to spot and we don't always know why we feel or think the way we do, so *how do you detect your self-limiting beliefs?*

To detect your self-limiting beliefs, you need to question your own behavior and ask why you react in a particular way. Try reflecting on a time you really wanted to do something, but you didn't do it, because something held you back. This could be something like singing at a karaoke in public or speaking to a group of people at a meeting. *What stopped you? Why didn't you do it?* A great way to work on this is to actually reflect on your journal and question yourself. This will help you to get to the heart of your beliefs. Someone who didn't sing at a karaoke, may believe they are a bad singer, and nobody will like their singing. But remember, plenty of people who are not experts in singing, sing at a karaoke for fun. It's not a serious activity, it's a social and fun activity. By recognizing this belief, you can start to make changes.

Once you can detect your own self-limiting beliefs, you can start to think about how you can push past your belief and make a new one. For example, if we refer to the karaoke example, a person may decide that they take the idea of sing at a karaoke too seriously. If they really want to sing at a karaoke, then they should do it. You can make a plan to move past this, so next time you have an opportunity to sing at a karaoke, you are going to do it because it is a fun activity and not a serious activity. You may start to tell yourself it doesn't matter whether or not you can sing.

Making a plan to alter your beliefs and overcome your fears can be a really refreshing experience and this helps you to push past limits. Planning ahead motivates you and once you've overcome the fear, you are no longer limited as you feel a sense of freedom. Start small at first, so that you don't overwhelm yourself. For example, sing with a friend or in a group if you are still too scared to sing alone, and then build up to singing alone.

How can I start to trust myself and instill self-belief?

If you have some automatic thoughts that stir-up self-doubt, you often don't even realize it's happening. Such negativity brings you down but when we automatically think in a specific way, it becomes nature to us.

Building up trust and self-belief is something we must work on as it doesn't come easy. *So, how do you start to do this?* First of all, you need to detect and unpack our beliefs as we discussed in the earlier sections. This is important because the first step is to understand ourselves and our beliefs.

Once you know and understand your beliefs, you need to make new ones. If we think of the karaoke example again, we need to change the fear of what other people think of our singing, to the idea that singing at a karaoke isn't serious singing anyway, it's just a thing to do for fun. As long as you have fun, the singing doesn't matter. Transform your beliefs into new ones and write them down. Detail them as being *my new core beliefs* and look at them every day. Writing them down is an important step because when you write something down, it's there, it's serious, and we think about it differently because we have essentially made a written contract with yourself.

The next step is to accept where you are now. Acceptance is important when you're trying to build up trust, because only then can you be honest with yourself. Think about where you are now and where you want to be.

You can then start to talk yourself into believing in yourself again. Yes, you did just read that correctly - you can talk yourself into believing in yourself. We've already talked previously about affirmations. They can be used to reprogram the mind and we can start to believe in ourselves again. Use your newly formed beliefs to shape everything you do from now on.

To move on further, you really need to start on getting rid of those negative thoughts and feelings, but this takes some time and work. Start by noting down any negative thoughts you have and then answer them with a positive thought. This is something you can do continuously and build on over time. Eventually, you'll start to refrain from negative thoughts and automatically think positively.

Set for yourself a new challenge. We fall into certain behavior patterns and when we stop trusting or believing in ourselves, we stop taking on challenges and learning new things. Start by setting a small challenge for yourself, push yourself to succeed in that challenge and you can see your confidence, trust and self-belief begin to grow.

Don't compare yourself to others. This again links to acceptance as you need to accept that you are you! We all like different things, and we all appear and sound differently, yet we feel the need to be someone else. Be yourself, accept yourself, and only ever try to improve yourself. You will always fail at being someone else because you are best at being you.

Set your own boundaries. When people lose belief and

trust in themselves, they start to do things they don't need or want to do because they feel obliged to. It's important that you set boundaries. Think about what you are and are not prepared to do. Fear often stops us from saying no and setting boundaries, but this is not a bad thing. A person who sets boundaries shows great leadership and assertiveness skills and this often builds a respectful culture. Ensure that you set both internal and external boundaries!

Self-doubt versus living with solid self-trust

While a certain amount of self-doubt is normal, it is important not to lose sight of what this can lead to. If your feelings and thoughts spiral out of control and you become anxious. This means it can become increasingly difficult to reel yourself back in as trust takes time to rebuild.

There is no question that too much self-doubt can lead to misery as we can end up living our life around it when we allow fear to take control of our life. If we trust ourselves, we take calculated risks and we are much happier. We are more likely to overcome barriers than simply being stopped, because we are programmed not to accept that. We can learn to see our barriers as a challenge rather than giving up and because we trust ourselves, we grow and develop as people.

When someone doesn't trust themselves, they stop controlling their own life. For instance, they lose accountability and blame others when things go wrong. A person who does not trust actually gives very little back to society. It's not necessarily their own fault, but their lack of trust stops them from contributing effectively as they distance themselves and shirk responsibilities.

People who trust themselves are open to improvements, have a strong sense of accountability, and they are ready for self-development and growth. They are influential figures because they make a difference and become well-respected. Imagine you're in the workplace and you're not sure how to handle a particular complaint by a customer. You know that the business gets a lot of work from this particular customer. *So, who do you go to?* Of course, you would go to the person who had made themselves a strong figure in the workplace – this is an important customer and you wouldn't hand them over to anyone. It has to be the most competent person who trusts themself and has your respect. You know that they will do their utmost to ensure that the issue is resolved and has little impact on the business as the customer will be looked after.

For a person who has a strong sense of self-trust, their confidence is more likely to improve too, because they begin to know what they want and become determined to get it. They treat themselves with the respect they deserve and by doing so, they demand it from others. We all deserve this, and we just have to find our pathway to building, developing and nurturing this trust.

Day 10-12 of your 30-day Recovery Plan

JOURNALING

How is your journaling going? Are you doing this every day? Journaling is great for capturing information, emptying our head and it's also useful if we just need to let off some steam. We've spent so much time focusing on behaviors, thought patterns and feelings, and let's face it, those things can become overwhelming.

Backtrack over the last three-five days and read your journal. At the end of each day, I want you to think about something positive – something you are proud of maybe. It doesn't have to be long but make a little note to remind you of this positive thing.

ACTIONABLE STEP

Take part in something that you would normally avoid. For example, if you usually avoid speaking at a team meeting, offer a five-minute talk. Note down the thoughts you have before and after. Think about how the experience has enriched you. It's fine to think about what you would do better, but also think about what you did well too.

ACTIVITY

1. Write a profile/description of a person you would trust. What would they do to gain your trust? How would they behave? What are their ethics? What type of person are they? This person is a reflection of you and your ethics. Are there any reasons why you shouldn't trust yourself? Remind yourself that you can trust yourself by keeping this description to hand.
2. Set yourself a challenge. Think of something that you really want to do, but for some reason, you haven't done it yet as a result of self-doubt.
3. Write some objectives – what do you need to do, to achieve this?
4. This is your first challenge, so don't overwhelm yourself but make it worthwhile. It has to be something that you really want to achieve in order to make sure you feel motivated.
5. Reflect on your achievements for the week. Write down your biggest win and share it with a friend or family member.

Chapter 5

Soothe Anxiety and Learn to "Recharge" Your Confidence

What do you think of when you hear the word soothe? For most people it means calm and ease. *What about the word, recharge?* For me, this is reviving something or bringing it back to life. Sometimes we need a confidence boost or recharge because maintaining confidence requires a lot of energy. It's like your cell phone, you can keep going for a long time, but eventually, your battery needs a rest and boost.

Soothing our anxiety and confidence is a skill we can learn ourselves. Think about when a baby is soothed. It's taken into a calming environment and pacified in some way until the baby is no longer twisting or crying. In order to soothe our anxieties, we need to feel calm and nurtured, but in order to do this we need to find out more about ourselves, explore our triggers and consider the actions that ease our thoughts and feelings. You should also be thinking about self-care as it's important to take care of both your body and mind, if you want to make progress. Learning to manage and boost our anxiety and confidence leads us on our journey to self-improvement.

How symptoms of anxiety could be knocking your confidence

If we suffer from anxiety, we are suffering an array of physical, mental and emotional symptoms. *Is it surprising to hear that this may be knocking your confidence?* Anxiety is when we become consumed by those feelings and reactions, and rather than controlling them, we allow them to control us. This is why anxiety and self-confidence are so closely related, because both can take over.

If we feel anxious, we have all sorts of irrational thoughts. We can start to avoid social situations and we can even have trouble sleeping even though you feel fatigued. Avoiding social gatherings and feelings of tiredness can start to knock our confidence. We might not feel like we are at our best and this can start to impact us as we don't feel good about ourselves. In addition, we could start to have other symptoms like panic attacks; we could struggle to concentrate, be irritable, agitated, and constantly feel worried. When we have such feelings, our brain is so occupied with the negatives that we stop caring for ourselves.

As soon as we stop caring for ourselves, we are in danger of heading on a downward spiral. We know we're not at our best. If we are exhausted, we may not look our best and we could struggle to concentrate. If we can't concentrate, we may not do our job to the best of our ability. It's not long before those thoughts begin to flare up, and we start bringing ourselves down. *If we make a single mistake, it means we're not good enough, right?* Of course not, but this is how we feel because we become irrational and we become harder on ourselves. It's emotionally and physically exhausting!

We don't always notice anxiety when it first starts to happen. That's because it often happens in a gradual way. As mentioned earlier, it makes us react in an irrational way; a way we can't explain at first. We can't help reacting in that specific way even though we know it's wrong. We could be super-emotional, extremely nervous, fidgeting, feel ill or sick in particular, or we could simply feel tense, restless, or panicked. Symptoms of anxiety are different for everyone and this makes it difficult to spot initially. Mindsets can change and sufferers can have a sense of danger occurring, or impending doom. Eventually the anxiety takes hold and it starts to control everything you do.

Some people suffer from a change in their breathing when they are anxious, or they sweat, and their heart rate increases. With these particular symptoms, many people find breathing into a paper bag useful, as it helps to regulate breathing and calm the nerves.

Confidence and anxiety are very closely linked. Imagine the symptoms discussed above – *can you imagine a person that suffers such terrible symptoms being able to portray themselves as being confident?* A person who feels anxious can damage their confidence, but a person who lacks confidence can also make themselves anxious too. They are both emotional reactions that are often fed by fear and both are completely normal, providing they do not spiral (Healthline, n.d.)[xxiii]. It's extremely important to work on confidence and anxiety too and recognize the signs at an early stage.

Both confidence and anxiety issues can actually be brought under control relatively easily in most cases, by making healthy choices and by spending some time working on ourselves, *but what happens if they spiral out of control before we take action? So, if we're overloaded or feel anxious, what can we do to recharge our confidence and keep those feelings of anxiousness at bay?*

Effective rest and stress-relief strategies that help you control your anxieties

If you're struggling with anxieties and stress now, and you feel they are starting to beat down your confidence, it's important to take action. For some reason, many of us are more of the 'suffer in silence' type, but that doesn't help anyone. If we need help or guidance, we can only get this if we admit we need assistance. *Good news!* There are some things you can do if you want to control your feelings and actions:

- Change how you think. This isn't as easy as it sounds but if you are a negative thinker, you really need to start changing how you think. Make a conscious decision to change this and spend time working on yourself. Set goals and think about how you want to improve and what you want or need from life.
- Find something that comforts you. We all have our home comforts or comfort zone, so think about what yours is. Now, we should never use our comfort zone to hide, but we can use it to rest and recharge. There's nothing wrong with taking a day off!
- Don't try to leap, take small steps. Any progress is

better than no progress, but it's important to focus on your goals. Nothing is going to transform you suddenly into a confident person, but you can make improvements and progress.

- Get plenty of rest. *How can anyone be expected to feel good if they don't take care and rest themselves?* Rest is so important to keep us healthy in both mind and body, so make sure you take your rest and get enough sleep as needed.
- We can boost our confidence and improve our anxiety by treating yourself. Have a facial, take a long soak in the tub, get your hair done, or do something else for yourself (treats in the home can be just as good). This can make us feel good or better, as personal hygiene and little treats can really improve our state of mind, and in turn, our motivation. It is also a great way to relieve stress.
- Accept your mistakes and don't hold onto the past. Remember that as a human being, we all make mistakes and use them to learn. Embrace them. Appreciate everything around you and live for the moment. Don't just accept mistakes, accept your past too, but live in and for the present. No regrets!

- Create a calming environment. Create a place you can relax and will feel comfortable and ensure you're away from things like coffee or loud music. You may wish to light candles, burn incense sticks or essential oils. You can rest, put up your feet and breathe deeply, while listening to calming music.
- Define what you want in life, make plans and don't give up. How will you achieve it? How will you get what you want? It's good to have plans and direction in your life, and a person who knows what they want is often more confident.
- Make healthy choices. Make sure you eat healthy snacks and stay hydrated. Things like fruit are ideal, and you should definitely drink plenty of water to help you stay hydrated. You could also try some yoga stretches too, as this is a very relaxing and soothing exercise that can help to clear your thoughts.
- Do something you don't usually do – something different or even a little spontaneous. Everyone likes a little bit of excitement in their life from time to time and this can really recharge and boost your confidence (Lifehack, n.d.)[xxiv].

How can resting and taking care of myself help my confidence?

Some of the ways to rest and refresh are so simple and yet so effective, but by now you'll be wondering how such things can help improve confidence and we may refer back to that word again... *Soothe.*

When we feel anxious or stressed, we can't possibly think straight. Our brain skims through our thoughts and feelings at a faster rate, and it becomes difficult to process information. This can lead to burn out, which means we feel drained of our energy. We are far from our best and this can increase the intensity of our anxiety and stress because when we are not feeling at our best, we make mistakes, we don't perform well, and we put extra pressure on ourselves because of this.

If we suffer from anxiety, we need to soothe the feelings that surround it. It's no good telling someone to 'get on with it' as this doesn't help. Someone with anxieties need to feel a sense of calm, they may need to be nurtured, and most importantly, they need to feel safe.

You can actually soothe your anxieties by resting and taking care of yourself, but we'll discuss this further, later.

If you don't get help, you will eventually hit burn out. This is because your anxieties will get worse if they aren't soothed. When someone hits burn out, it can take much longer to recover, so it's best to prevent getting to that stage. Our bodies and minds tire, as anxieties tend to drain our energy. It's so important to rest well in order to function efficiently. When we are well-rested, feeling good and thinking straight, it helps us to feel confident and happy.

Many people talk about resting to recharge their batteries, but it is possible to also recharge your confidence with rest, and a little positivity. Being in a peaceful environment can calm the mind and your confidence will improve as the mind clears of its thoughts. If you struggle to rest well, try deep breathing or meditation.

For example, let's think about meditating…

By meditating daily, we can rest our whole body. We can also follow guided meditations that help us focus on the positive things, avoid anxiety and improve our mindset and the way we are thinking.

Ultimately, resting gives you the energy boost you need to carry on with your life, drive forward and work on your confidence. You can introduce many things into your daily routine that will boost your energy and in turn, your confidence.

Your resting needs to be quality. You need somewhere peaceful that you can kick back and relax, even close your eyes. Being away from false light and in a quiet environment can also help. Rest doesn't necessarily mean sleep, but sleep is important, so ensure you get enough sleep through the night. Maybe you just need a quick nap to recharge and that's fine too!

How can I make changes to boost my energy levels?

There's nothing worse than having low energy. It can

affect mood, motivation and even concentration. Having good levels of energy can really help to boost your confidence and this can generally make you feel better. There are some things you can do to boost your energy levels and seven of those are listed below.

1. Having a routine that includes rest and sleep time can improve your health and wellbeing, which will certainly boost your energy. Yes, we've already mentioned sleep but it's so important. We'll cover routines in the later chapters.
2. You should also have breakfast and keep well hydrated, by drinking plenty of water. Again, we've covered water but again, this is vital.
3. If you struggle to switch off in the evening, you should use your journal to empty your mind and just write down whatever is in your head so you can deal with this the next day.
4. Exercising first thing in the morning is also a proven method to help you boost your energy levels. A brisk walk first thing can be a great way to set yourself up for the day and boost your energy.

5. Many people enjoy making more mindful changes, like meditation and breathing exercises. Reflecting in your journal and on your day can also be really valuable, especially if you focus on the positives.
6. You can also use affirmations to positively reinforce each day. Write them out on a post-it note and stick them somewhere you can review them every day.
7. Other people enjoy reading or writing too, as this is a great way to relax and recharge. Read something you can really get into and write whatever is on your mind.

If you make small lifestyle changes like the seven listed above, you will notice a difference to your energy levels almost instantly. Boosting energy levels can be really effective and when we feel energized, it generally makes us feel happier. You should consider making small changes as smaller changes are more effective than larger changes and they are more likely to be successful.

Take small steps because each step is long-lasting progress that you can be proud of Approach these changes with an open mind and give each one a try.

You have nothing to lose!

Day 13 – 15 of your 30-Day Recovery Plan

JOURNALING

Do you journal in the morning or evening?

When you journal in the evening, you can empty your head before bed, reflect on your day, make plans for tomorrow or further into the future, and consider things you have learned or have made you happy. It's a chance to empty your head and often people who journal in the evening, sleep better. Some people prefer to do this the next morning, when they have had more time to digest the information and that can work too, but remember that the mind isn't always fully awake when you first wake up, so you may need to wait until you've got dressed and had some breakfast before you begin.

Don't forget to keep journaling and ensure you spend some time reflecting on your days and experiences!

ACTIONABLE STEP

In this chapter we've looked at confidence, and we've also focused on taking chances, reducing anxiety and boosting your energy levels.

You have 3 actionable steps for each day, to help you boost your energy levels:

1. Plan a new routine that includes staying hydrated and exercise first thing.
2. Arrange a social event with friends.
3. Visit Youtube and try out a guided meditation that focuses on positivity, confidence or success.

If you want to make changes, it's important to take positive action.

ACTIVITY

Your activity in this chapter is to try free writing and this requires some level of commitment from you. This is different to journaling, because you can write anything, but you don't have to think (in fact it's better if you don't), and it doesn't have to be structured. It's a great way to spark your creativity:

- When you go to bed in the evening, leave a notepad and pen next to your bed.
- Set your alarm 30 minutes earlier than usual (sorry, but this part is crucial. You can do it).
- As soon as your alarm bell rings, pick up your pad and start writing whatever you feel like writing. Remember this is free writing, and you shouldn't think, just write anything that springs to mind. You can make sense of all later, as the idea is that you're writing without being fully awake, so it's from your subconscious.
- Write for between 10-20 minutes.
- Try 5 minutes of meditation afterwards and do some Yoga stretches if possible.
- Once you're dressed and have had breakfast, go back to your writing and read what you've written. *Does anything catch your eye?* You may be able to use some of this for various reasons – for creative purposes or as a to-do list / reminder.

Free writing is great for creative people as it can really encourage your creative spark. Some people have stressed that they aren't creative people, but then they flourish in this exercise. Give it a try! Being creative could mean you're creative in your ideas or in business, so don't assume it has to be arts, crafts or writing. Being creative is so much more, it's an expansion of our ideas and it's something that we are all capable of. Don't sell yourself short until you've tried it – you may even be surprised!

Chapter 6

Check Your Self-Image to Eliminate Tendencies of Comparison

How do you feel about your own image? Are you happy with it? You'll be surprised how many people say *no!* It's human nature to form opinions, we do this automatically. When we open a magazine or watch the television, we may wish we had hair like the lady on the shampoo advert or are hope that we are as thin as a certain movie star. That's because we have the consistent need to compare ourselves to others or wish for those things we don't have.

If we keep focusing on what we don't have, it's hard to remain positive and happy. It's just as important to focus on what we *do* have. The way we feel about ourselves, and our need to compare ourselves can become unhealthy. It's certainly bad for our state of mind. If a person isn't happy with their self-image, then they should change it. But you need to concentrate on being more like *'you'*, not in the image of someone else.

What do we mean by 'self', what is self-image, and how is it formed and developed?

The word self ultimately refers to us. It's our opinion of who we are and what we look like. The idea of 'self' is talking or thinking about our own self. We all have opinions and ideas of our self, as we know who we are and what we're about… *Or do we?* Although it's normal to form an opinion of our self, we are known to be harsh. Sometimes, we aren't necessarily positive and while we might think highly of ourselves at a certain point of our life, this doesn't mean we'll always feel like that. As humans we have high and low points throughout our life.

What we think of ourselves, isn't necessarily a reflection of what others think as we are programmed to criticize ourselves. When we suffer from confidence issues, it can be really difficult to see the positives, especially when referring to our self. While we may think we are weak in nature, others may see us as being strong and independent. Perception is everything when it comes to referring to one's self. That brings us nicely onto self-image, because what we see in the mirror isn't necessarily what someone thinks. We may not like one of our facial features, like our nose, but others may think it suits our face. A person with an eating disorder may see someone as overweight when in fact, other people see someone thin and struggling.

It's reasonable to suggest that our ideas of our self and self-image are formed by our own perceptions. This can depend heavily on our thoughts, beliefs, actions and emotions.

Have you ever heard anyone or even yourself say, 'I'm a mess,' when they are feeling upset? Well, we are referring to how we feel because we have been crying or at least feel like it. This reflects what we perceive on the outside too because we view the world differently when we are feeling emotional – we could feel an array of emotions, positive or negative, and each of these would influence our perception of how we feel. This may not always be apparent to other people as when we tell someone we're a mess, we might be on the inside, but to others we may look okay on the outside.

Sometimes, it is reflected in our exterior appearance. If we are fatigued, we look withdrawn and our eyes may appear sunken and have dark rings surrounding the socket. A person who we are close to may notice this, but sometimes we hide how we feel by slapping on some make-up to hide the tiredness. For some people, this boosts their confidence and they are able to portray a positive self-image. But this doesn't work for everyone!

The opinions we form when it comes to ourselves are

difficult to explain because we are individual. How we feel about our self is down to our own personal beliefs and automatic thoughts. We make assumptions, and because we are talking about us, we feel our judgments are justified. *Who knows us better than we know ourselves?* Well, that's a very good question.

In truth, we form opinions based on our beliefs, thoughts and feelings, but as these things can change and develop over time, so does our opinion of ourselves. For example, a woman in her early twenties with a good job may feel great, but she may then get married and have a child and as we head into the later twenties to early thirties, she may feel differently about herself. Maybe her career is on hold, she's not as fit or thin as she used to be, and she feels starved of the intelligent company she was a part of for so long. Those things are less important to her now, but that doesn't mean she doesn't miss them, even though she wouldn't change the path she chose. This could have a detrimental effect on how she feels about herself, but also, we can't forget the 'mom-guilt' she'll also feel right now. She became a mother and it was the best thing that ever happened to her... so *why does she crave intelligent company? Why is she bothered about her looks, weight and fitness? Her career is only on hold for now until the most precious thing in her life goes to school or grows up, so why does she feel like she's lost?*

For some women, they would instantly chastise themselves for feeling that way and brand themselves a bad mother. Yet, when we don't work or have a career, we can also be seen as a poor role model. That's right, we can't win!

The most important consideration to ask yourself here is, *what's right for me or us?* When you build your confidence, you will choose your path with ease and overcome these barriers because you will only be concerned with the greater good for you and your family, and not the judgments placed on you by society or individuals. Such things will be insignificant to you because they have no impact on your life.

Over time, those things that are important to us change,

and this alters how we feel about our self and how we view our self-image. There still could be part of us that wants that something we once had, but as we evolve, our priorities change. As we move on in our life, we experience new things and we change our beliefs. As we hit the bumps in the road on the way, things become more important while others become less. Someone who isn't bothered about their weight may find they have a health condition and suddenly, they may realize that they have to change their diet and lose weight. This will totally change the way they feel about themselves. Failing or relapsing will also cause depressive or negative thoughts and we could beat ourselves down in our mind.

While our ideas and opinions of ourselves comes from us, let's not forget that sometimes there are external factors that shape how we feel and think. We are often forced into comparing ourselves to others, but this can lead to feelings of inadequacy. By comparing ourselves, we can actually cause ourselves to feel down and depressed.

Have you ever looked in a magazine at an image of a model wearing that new lipstick you want or a swimsuit you love, but you feel inadequate because you know you can't compare to her?

Stop this, right now!

How comparing ourselves makes us unhappy and gives our confidence a bashing

Society likes to organize everything and everyone, so it's normal for us to put ourselves and everything we do into little boxes or categories. While healthy competition is normal, doing this to an extreme can be harmful because it causes us to constantly judge and compare ourselves with others. We are generally happier if we are ourselves, so it's important to just be yourself.

If you don't want to wreck your confidence and self-esteem, then you shouldn't compare yourself to others.

If we refer back to the swimsuit example in the earlier section, we already feel depressed because we know that we're never going to look like the image of the perfect model wearing it. It was made for her. The question is, *why do we want to look exactly like her?* If we all appeared the same, wore exactly the same clothes and were shaped in the same way, we would lead very boring lives.

Comparing ourselves to others makes us unhappy but it's something we do as human beings. It's a learned behavior that we pick up from a young age and it creates a disconnection between ourselves and others. It means we follow social norms in society in an attempt to fit in with others and blend in well, yet this very thing makes us feel inadequate. This is because it's not really us as we aren't being our true selves. There is always someone out there that is doing it better or looks better and this makes us feel like we are not good enough. We are much happier if we are true to our self. Although we do not necessarily learn uniqueness, it is vibrant, and it stands out. We should therefore view a confident person as being unique in a positive way, because we are taught to blend in and follow social norms, being unique is something we have to warm up to. We have to work on this.

If you want to be happy, you must change this behavior right now and stop comparing yourself to others. This will help you to rebuild and instill a new-found confidence. The word unique means to be individual and different. Someone who is unique is not like anyone else, so this is often something we must discover and become comfortable with on our own. Once we do this, our confidence can grow and thrive.

If you want to stop comparing yourself to others, there are a few things you must do:
- Remember that things aren't always what they seem. The lady in the swimsuit may have had the swimsuit fitted and her pictures airbrushed professionally. Nobody is perfect.
- Cling to your self-worth and remember that it's what's on the inside that matters. You are your own person.
- Do what's right for you! Just because others are

doing a certain thing, doesn't necessarily mean that thing is right for you, right now. Don't worry about what others are doing just focus on what you are doing and what your strengths are.
- Remember that we all have weaknesses as we can't possibly be good at everything. Give yourself a break!
- Know what you want! Think about your own interests and what you like to do. *What are you good at?*
- Be realistic. It's no good placing expectations on yourself that you are never going to achieve. Always be reasonable with your expectations.
- Always focus on the positives. It's not always easy to be positive about yourself but you should certainly focus on the good points.
- Be unique and be happy! Individuality is a positive thing so use that and embrace it.
- While it's normal to have healthy competition, remember that everything doesn't have to be. Just simply aim to be the best person you can be!
- Find out your purpose. Think about what you want in life and what matters to you.
- Enjoy yourself! Give yourself permission to enjoy

life, do what you love and take care of yourself (AGATHANGELOU, 2015)[xxv].

Self-esteem and confidence in a digital age

There are many pros and cons to social media when it comes to self-esteem and confidence. While social media can be used to post motivational quotes, affirmations, success stories and adverts that will help improve self-esteem and confidence, just like the paper-based media, there are things that can smash it too.

You might feel really bad about yourself. Maybe you don't have much money for Christmas as you're going through a difficult time, and people start posting how many presents they have got for their family or how much money they have spent, this will not make you feel good. It sends you on a spiral. Again, people can modify images and post picture-perfect lives that you can only dream to have. You need to be aware that not everything on social media is true. The lady two blocks away who bakes the most amazing cookies and appears to be the most amazing mom with the most well-behaved, clean and happy kids you've ever seen is probably not all she seems. That's because social media is filtered, and people only allow you to see what they want you to see.

Isn't it a great feeling when you finally get to see an honest post, video, or picture on social media that shows life's little imperfections? That's because it's real! Life is full of imperfections and all those posts, images and videos that make you feel inadequate are not a true reflection or representation of life.

Recent studies have shown that regular Facebook users have shown a decline in mental health, and self-esteem. A recent study considered the detrimental and negative impact this can have on our mental health. One study in particular explored patterns between different Facebook habits and found that of the many 1,104 people who participated, the ones who engaged regularly with Facebook ended up with deteriorated mental health, felt body shame and lower self-esteem (Petersen, 2017)[xxvi].

Regardless of the negative impact social media appears to have on several people, we continue to return to it and use it. *Why is that?* Well, social media has grown into a huge media platform and now everyone uses it, including businesses. You can use social media to communicate, to sell, to buy, and to advertise your products and services. Students can use it to communicate with classmates and complete study projects and you can even use social media for research purposes too. Wherever we go, we can rarely escape the clutches of social media, and that's because there are many benefits to this too.

We should, however, control our usage, take breaks as required, and change our own thoughts, beliefs and feelings when using this to enable us to remain effective and efficient when using it. We need to be aware of the effects of social media and allow ourselves to take back control, without letting it affect our self-esteem and confidence. Sometimes simply being aware that such things can cause problems can allow us to move forward.

Day 16-18 of your 30-day recovery plan

JOURNALING

Journaling plays a large part in your recovery, so hopefully you're still doing this daily. While you may have very little to write on some days, you may have lots to write on others. Don't worry, there's no right or wrong way to do this!

Just for the next three days, you should monitor your social media usage in your journal. The main point of this is to raise your awareness – don't use it more, don't use it less, just use it as you would on a typical day. For fun, before you begin, estimate how long you think you spend on social media, in one day.

Social media can really impact how we feel and sometimes, we don't even realize the affect it has over us. Over the next three days, note down the times you use social media in your journal so that you can monitor this and answer one question – *how do you feel after your social media session?*

Did you estimate how much time you spend on social media in total in one day, correctly?

ACTIONABLE STEP

In this chapter we've talked about self-image, our view of our self, and things that can lower our self-esteem and confidence, like social media.

You have 3 actionable steps for each day, to help you boost your energy levels:

1. List three things you think about your 'self' and 'self-image' Keep it positive!
2. List your strengths and three things you are proud of.
3. Write down three things you would like to change or achieve in your life.
4. Study these and write some goals that focus on how you can use your opinions of yourself and your strengths to achieve those things.

ACTIVITY

Your activity in this chapter is to explore your 'self' and self-image.

- Write a list about yourself – positive and negative.

- Look at the negative – *why do you believe those things about you? Think* about your childhood or any influences in your life. This could be your parents' beliefs, societal beliefs, social media etc...
- Look at yourself in the mirror. *What do you see?*
- Write down anything you would change.
- Now ask another person, someone you trust, *what are three positive and negative things they would say about you?*
- Ask them about your image too – *how do you look (tired, happy etc...)?*
- Analyze this and think about anything you would change. *What would you change? How?*
- Think about how your own personal beliefs impact how you view yourself and your image. *Are they irrational or rational? Realistic or unrealistic?*

Chapter 7

Uncover the Negative Stories You Tell Yourself to Rewrite Your Inner Dialogue

In the previous chapter we talked about beliefs, but most of the time, even if we don't really acknowledge it, our beliefs are based on a story. *Have you ever talked yourself out of doing something?* Say you're invited to party, but before you go, you've talked yourself into believing that you're not going to have a good time, and you don't. Then you feel a sense of satisfaction, because you were right, you didn't have a good time. You know things could've gone very differently had you been in a positive mindset and that's because we control our own stories.

Our life is made up of stories. Our stories make us who we are. Stories are based on our experiences and beliefs, as they are things that we tell ourselves within our minds, using our internal dialogue. Remember that stories aren't always the whole truth. That party you went to that was lame, but several people at that party had a good time; you had a lame time because you'd talked yourself out of wanting to go. You shaped that story, but *why did you shape that in a negative way?*

We all have a story to tell our self, but how accurate are they?

In the previous chapters we've talked about self-esteem and confidence, and how we can be harsh on ourselves. That's all still true, but until we change our beliefs, we will continue to have the same thought and behavior patterns. Our stories are often shaped by those beliefs and impacted by our experiences in life.

We do have to be wary when believing our internal stories as sometimes what we tell ourselves aren't wholly true. It's not like we intentionally lie to ourselves. The inner dialogue that tells you stories is not your friend but a replication of your self-doubt. Your internal dialogue never stops, and it narrates everything we see, hear, and experience. The problem is that your mind can manipulate the information however it wants. The information can then be adapted and filtered as it's there to comfort you and make you feel safe. For example, if a dog bit you and you subsequently became afraid of dogs, your inner dialogue isn't going to admit that. It would tell you that you just don't like dogs anymore as it wouldn't confirm the fear. If you went to visit someone with a dog, perhaps you may say that you don't really like dogs, or they don't like you. If you were feeling really defensive you might even say you're allergic to them. That's because your inner dialogue tries to soothe and protect you. This reveals that your inner voice isn't in line with reality.

Your inner voice could become harmful, especially if your confidence or self-esteem are low. It's going to be destructive and it will try to wear you down. *Is that inner voice really what you want to lead you in everything you do?* If not, it's time to change that inner voice. We need to change its reactions, responses and even its tone. We are no longer going to accept such a negative force to guide us!

We can't stop our inner dialogue, but we do have the power to make deep changes to our mind that impacts the way we think, act and feel. By simply being aware we can change how we respond to our inner voice. We can learn to quieten the voice when it's being ridiculous, persuade it to think in a different way, and remove its power. You can do this by ignoring it, filtering it and proving it wrong. You can also distract yourself from it and clear your mind, until you can think clearly. Breathing exercises and meditation can help with this (Bokhari, 2019)[xxvii].

How important are our internal stories?

Internal stories aren't all bad and there's no denying that our stories make us who we are. We can use positive stories and experiences to shape our future too. Without our stories, we could be a completely different person as we may have made different life choices. Stories are pivotal points in our life that are instrumental in how we think, feel and act today. For instance, someone who battled a mental health issue and now helps others do so, would be really passionate about their work. People would trust them because of their honesty and firsthand experience. A person who was bullied at school and completely turned their life around and now advocates for victims would again be an asset as they would be trustworthy and capable of helping others who are being bullied. They would give hope to others. A person who suffered financial difficulties such as a bankruptcy, and then developed a million dollar company would certainly be listened to in relation to financial advice because there are so many who could identify with them. Furthermore, due to that person's experience, they would feel empathy and understanding towards their audience.

You can control the stories we use to shape who we are, and you can also choose how you portray or use them. This doesn't mean we should lie, as we should always be honest, but we, need to use them in a positive way so that they can be effective. If we refer again to the bullying example, it is much more powerful to be a success and help others as a result of enduring suffering as a victim, than it is to remain a victim all of our life. Remember, people love success stories.

Our internal stories play a huge role in how confident we are or how confident we appear. We can make the change to ensure that we make the most of that. Above, we discussed success stories and if we have a story to tell that leads to success, it makes us feel good. It's a justification of why we are successful today. It shows us in a positive light and can portray us as strong people who know our own minds and made it through hardships. Our stories are important because they connect us to others, they remind us of who we are and they provide the boost we need to increase our confidence and self-esteem, because they remind us of the journey we've taken to be who we are today.

How to observe your inner dialogue and rewrite it

It's official, you're not crazy. That little voice that twitters away in your head is really there. It's your inner dialogue, telling you what to do and nagging you. But how often do you listen, or do you tell it to be quiet?

So, how do we observe our inner dialogue? When something is chattering away inside your head regularly, you get used to it. It becomes difficult to pinpoint it, so at first you will really need to listen to yourself. *What does it say?*

Your inner dialogue is going to occur every time you're faced with a decision as well, but over time you can change it, as when an emotion or action is triggered. It's a type of automatic thought that you can't prevent. Raising awareness is a huge part of this book, and that's because awareness lays the foundation for improvement. We are on a journey to improve our confidence, and that means we need to explore our feelings, actions and thoughts. Listen for your inner dialogue.

Sometimes, our inner voice is not telling us anything positive. It could be telling you you're not good at something or you need to avoid that social event. This voice represents all your fears, doubts and insecurities. We need to learn to reshape this, and we need to investigate why our voice is saying negative things.

If you want to get to the bottom of this, you should log the events that initiate the automatic thoughts. Write down what happened, what your voice was telling you, and why you reacted in such a way. Ask yourself why your mind is telling you to react in such a way.

Negative automatic thoughts are unhealthy for us. If we are constantly replaying scenarios, beating ourselves up or thinking about mistakes, we will knock our own confidence and self-esteem for sure. This means it's imperative to question our thoughts, feelings and actions. If you're reacting, or have just reacted negatively, it's important to clear your mind before you move any further. You can relax, take a bath, read a book, exercise, take a walk, or meditate. Once your mind is clear, you're ready to begin to take action.

Take a look at the events you've noted down and ask how you would like to react. Also think about how you can overcome those negative feelings. *What can you do to prevent feeling, reacting or thinking this? What would soothe your inner voice?*

Think about what is causing you to think this way. Reflect on the pivotal points and stories in your life that shape who you are. *What belief is responsible for how you think/feel/act right now?* Once you've worked this out, you can rewrite your story in the essence it was intended. You can change it around and flip it into something positive. Form your new beliefs based on your new story. Start to harness your internal complimenting voice. This is the voice that observes the positive things you do. You also need to think about what motivates you, from within. If your internal voice was talking to you, what would it say to motivate you?

Develop an internal tone and be firm. Remember when you were a child and how mom talked to you? She used different tones, right? We have the upset tone, the disappointed tone, the happy and excited tone, the angry tone, etc... Develop your own tone inside your head. Be firm with yourself and assertive when you have to give yourself a good talking to and be upbeat when it's time to motivate yourself. If you're using those tones inside your head, you can channel them to achieve the desired effect.

Remember, internal dialogue is powerful, and it belongs to us – those are our words. We can rewrite it and use it to forge and strengthen confidence and self-esteem by challenging our stories and revising our beliefs. When you make changes to your thoughts, feelings and actions you really begin to make your confidence flourish.

To rewrite your internal dialogue, you need to question it. We don't live our lives based on the opinions of others, but we do need to accept that sometimes, we won't agree with what our internal voice says. If someone tells us that we can lose weight if we follow a certain diet, we want proof. With that in mind, we should never take our internal voice at face value, because it's only worth listening to if it's making valid points. When your voice starts chatting on, make sure it's being relevant, and its claims are founded. If not, you need to hush it up – be stern. *Is it a justified point? Is it constructive or argumentative? Does your voice have any evidence that backs up its claim?* In order to rewrite your internal dialogue, you need to be able to quieten it down before it gains momentum. If your inner voice talks to you in a negative way, remind it that it needs to be positive. In time, your voice will learn to react in a productive way that is of benefit to you, rather than hindering.

Day 19-21 of your 30-day Recovery Plan

JOURNALING

You've now had 18 previous days to journal. If you're struggling with ideas of what to write, really concentrate on the decisions you've made. Think about what led you to that decision.

REFLECTION: Look at your journal for the last three days and consider anything that you've done that triggered negative thoughts.

Think about your belief system – why did you react in a negative way?

Think about your ideal – how would you like to react?

Think about your story – what story from your past impacted the way you reacted?

ACTIONABLE STEP

Rewrite a pivotal story in your life. A pivotal story is something that changed your life and you've altered what you do or how you think ever since. It's a turning point. For example, a woman could have a child, and suddenly find that they develop stronger career aspirations and may want to change their job, progress or even go back to education so that they can make a better life. Having a child made her want more and aspire to be more.

Our lives are full of pivotal stories that shaped the path we have taken so far. Sometimes we do things because of the way we've been treated, to prove somebody or ourselves wrong, or because of an event that has occurred and either inspired or motivated us. If something happens that has pushed us into action, then it's a pivotal story.

What're your pivotal stories?
1. Think of three stories that have influenced your life. They must include a pivotal point. They can be positive or negative and you should ask yourself, what did I learn?
2. Reflect on the goals you wrote in the previous chapter.
3. Rewrite your stories based on what you've learned or achieved and consider how you can use them to shape your future and achieve your goals.

ACTIVITY

Your activity in this chapter is to challenge your beliefs and internal voice.
- Write down your core beliefs. If you aren't sure what your beliefs are, reflect on your journal and pinpoint how your beliefs or life events contribute to the way we view things. Think about why you believe that/think that/feel that/react like that and then you

will begin to unpack your beliefs.
- Write down your belief, and if it's negative, challenge it. For example, if you come from a poor background, you may think that you are destined to never make money. You need to flip that around – *who says you can't make money? Who says you can't be rich/confident/happy?* You will find that a lot of your beliefs are unfounded.
- Once you've done this, devise a list of your new core beliefs in life.
- Now you have your beliefs, use them to challenge your inner voice. If your inner voice says anything negative; anything that doesn't resonate with your core beliefs, challenge it. From now on, your core beliefs shape you, your beliefs, and your stories.

A confident person has strong core beliefs that they live by and their stories make them who they are, based on these values. It takes some getting used to, but congratulations, because once you have, you've made important progress towards improving your confidence and self-esteem.

Chapter 8

Build Self-Care Routines that Remind You of Your Worth

We often tell our friends or relatives that they should take care of themselves. This is something that you've probably been told yourself too from time to time, or maybe more often. When you're stressed or feel low, it becomes increasingly difficult to think about yourself. We may feel we don't have time to take a walk, spend a little extra time relaxing in the tub, or maybe we don't have the time or money to go to the salon or spa. In truth, we're the first people to warn others to take care of themselves and yet many people are not used to practicing what they preach. If you want to build your confidence and the feeling of self-worth, you need to change that and building a self-care routine is a step in the right direction!

Self-care and why we need it

There's been some hype surrounding the idea of self-care over the last few years. There are many coaches, counsellors, doctors, other health care professionals and even workplaces that focus on supporting or encouraging individuals to look after or care for themselves. When we have busy lives – maybe we work, run a business, have children, care for an elderly relative or are studying, and we pour our heart and soul into it, this often comes at a cost. The cost of neglecting yourself because we switch into a machine mode, and we seem to sacrifice self-care. This could mean that we become run down, depressed, less efficient, or even sick as a result. Spending some time caring for ourselves can prevent this!

Self-care obviously means to care for one's self. Sometimes we don't look after ourselves as we should, but ask yourself, *if we don't look after ourselves, who will? Who better to know exactly what we need, than us?* We are the best people to care for ourselves because we know exactly what we need to heal, regroup and refocus.

We can look after ourselves by getting enough sleep, drinking plenty of water, meditating, eating nutritious and healthy food, exercising and by treating ourselves to occasional treats like a facial or a visit to the salon, to help us feel good or relaxed. *But why is this so difficult?*

For most of us, it's in our nature to put others first and ourselves last. This is not a negative trait of ours, however, this can lead on a path to self-neglect. When we don't have a lot of time, we neglect ourselves further and then we stop listening to our own needs and kind of block them out. This also becomes natural to us because it's easy to get into the habit of ignoring ourselves. This again links back to the idea of self-worth, because indirectly, the care of ourselves is always something that we feel justified to sacrifice, above all else.

It's really important that we take care of ourselves and stop neglecting the need for self-care because there are so many benefits. We are often more productive, motivated, and happy when we care for ourselves, so not caring for ourselves is counterproductive. If we care for ourselves, we tend to be more focused and it gives us that valuable reflection time to listen to our mind. That way, we know what we want in life.

Let's also remember that self-care can also help us to keep our body and mind healthy. This can help to improve our confidence and you will soon start to realize your own self-worth.

That little voice inside of us that whispers to us whether we deserve something or not, often tells us we shouldn't spend time, energy, or money on ourselves.

We don't deserve or need it, but this is wrong. We do! We have already considered the benefits of self-care, but we do actually need it to function effectively. Self-care can fuel so many other positive changes in our life. It's the foundation for us to grow. It's time to let go of everything that bogs us down by showing ourselves a little bit of appreciation.

Many people wonder how they can possibly fit in self-care, but self-care doesn't have to be too time consuming. You can spend an extra ten minutes in the tub relaxing, give yourself a homemade facial or meditate for five-ten minutes each day. The easiest and most effective way is to build it into your schedule. You schedule in work time and other activities, so reap the benefits and schedule in self-care.

You won't be disappointed!

How to boost your self-worth

Self-worth is how you value yourself and this is something that many people generally struggle with.

We get so used to putting ourselves last and this prevents us from valuing ourselves as we don't really think about the things that we're good at.

If we're honest, as human beings we often focus on the negative things that happen rather than the positive. This isn't good for our mind and body, and we have to learn to reframe our thoughts to think of the positive things: *what do we do well? What are we good at? What good things happened?*

How can we do this?

Thoughts are automatically formed in our mind, so it isn't always easy to change our thought patterns, but awareness is the first step. If you aware of those negative thoughts that are punishing your self-worth, then you are taking the first step towards your transformation.

People often judge themselves on their net worth, appearance, social circles, career, and achievements, but these are false, and if we simply judge ourselves on these things, we are setting ourselves up for failure. These things do not necessarily decide whether or not we're a worthy person or determines how valuable we are. It's time to take a step back and evaluate ourselves on a higher level, and we must ensure we don't get caught up worrying about how many friends or followers someone has on social media. Although this could indicate popularity, this does not indicated value or worth.

When evaluating your self-worth, you should be thinking about the things that matter most and the qualities that truly define you as a person as they can boost how you feel about yourself. Think about happiness, positivity, compassion, kindness, respect, and other personality traits that make you who you are. You should also think about identifying your voice and how we control this. We've talked about our inner voice and how it's great at telling us the negative things, but it needs to be managed in an effective way. Whenever your voice starts twittering on, pause it, question it, tell it to shut up. You should then remind yourself why this is false and just how valuable you are. Then you can move on.

Don't forget that you are not defined by the people who love you, it's the love we feel for ourselves. If we do value our very being, we will feel better, and typically we'll have better relationships too. Caring for others and being cared for is important for our emotional wellbeing (Ackerman, 2019)[xxviii].

Feeling well-cared for versus feeling worthy

We all like feeling loved and cared for. We allow the love and praise from others take make us feel good and encourage us, but this simply isn't enough. Regardless of the relationships we have, we should still feel good and be able to stand on our own feet. It's so important to be able to encourage ourselves and we must remember that other people do not define who *we* are.

If we allow the love of others to define us, we are putting our lives in their hands and this is a mistake. It can actually damage relationships because in truth, if we don't have love and respect for ourselves, we will never have love and respect for anyone else. A healthy sense of self-worth will help you to maintain a healthy, mutual relationship with others and this love will be satisfying and stable. Of course, we do love people and if anything happens, it can make us feel low. We may even feel like part of us is missing and this is normal, but we must have boundaries.

To have an equal relationship, both parties must feel worthy and have both respect and love for themselves. In order for a relationship to be happy and survive, both people must feel self-worth. If only one person has little self-worth, it can be very draining on the other person. The person who has self-worth can help to the lift the spirits of the person without self-worth, but this can only ever be a temporary fix, because we can only lift another person's self-worth for so long as it's draining. If we have to maintain both our own self-worth and another's, it can make us feel low as we spend so much time and energy on the other person. If neither have self-worth, it can be an unhappy or sometimes destructive relationship.

If both parties feel a strong sense of self-worth, they will have a mutual love and respect for one another. When you feel appreciation for yourself, it's easier to feel appreciation for each other. This is what a healthy relationship is all about. Together, they will bring happiness and warmth. Even at times if one is a little low, they can boost each other but this is equal – one does not drain the other.

Being cared for is still important and it's kind of a basic need of human nature, it just shouldn't be the only thing that boosts us. Others are attracted to us if we are positive and confident on our own, but others can also help us to be even better.

The ability to show up confidently in your life comes from within, from this self-worth and you can do this by:
- Stop comparing yourself to others.
- Ensuring you feel self-love and respect, without relying on relationships.
- Considering your own true value based on things that are important to you or the things that matter.
- Reflecting, organizing, and reframing your thoughts.

- Spending time resting your mind and body (getting enough sleep or meditating for example).

Doing these things can send you on the right path and help you turn up confident and focused, daily (Ackerman, 2019)[xxix].

Are hobbies a type of self-care?

This question is down to your discretion and your personal idea of self-care. Many people stop their hobbies when they feel down or under pressure because they feel like they don't have the time. This is one of the worst things we can do, because if we stop doing the things we like, we end up feeling worse and we're setting on a downward spiral. Now we've talked about self-care already, and many people wonder whether doing some activities that they enjoy or are good at would pass as self-care. It absolutely does!

It's easy to lose sight of ourselves, and if we stop doing those activities we love or enjoy, it's often because our confidence is dipping. That's exactly why it's important to do those things we love and enjoy. Doing these things makes us happy, and happiness makes us feel good. This is when we are at our best and are more likely to feel confident.

If you enjoy something like swimming, crafts, or reading then you should do it, because being happy is good for your soul and it's actually the ultimate example of self-care. It's your individual method of escape. *What better way to make ourselves happy?* It's uplifting.

Days 22-24 of your 30-day Recovery Plan

JOURNALING

You're really getting on with your journaling now and that's great. Over the next three days, you should focus on self-care. Note down any self-care activities you do and think about the ones that are the most beneficial to you. *Why?*

ACTIONABLE STEP

Choose a self-care activity for the next three days – it can be as small or as big as you like. Take a longer bath, meditate for 5 minutes, or something even more extravagant – you choose!

Then answer the questions below:
- After my self-care activity, how did I feel?
- What did I do afterwards that was productive and was I more productive than usual?

ACTIVITY

At the end of your three days, reflect on your self-care activities.

Which self-care activity is the most effective for you?
Did it make you more productive?
Which self-care activity did you enjoy the most and why?
What self-care activity would you like to try in the future?

Self-care needs to be consistent in order for it to be effective. You can reap the benefits, which includes increased productivity and clearer thinking if you take the time to do this regularly. Nobody is suggesting that you take hours out of your day, but small rewards are key.

*Finally, make a plan to incorporate self-care into your daily routine.

Chapter 9

Observe Improvements You've Made to Start Giving Yourself Credit for Progress

Have you ever said *congratulations...* to yourself?

We are terrible at giving ourselves the credit we deserve. It makes us feel awkward and we also don't want to give the impression of being over-confident. It's certainly difficult to celebrate or sometimes even acknowledge our own improvements, because we simply don't always notice. This may sound silly, but while we pay attention to the achievements of others that we care about, we don't necessarily think about ourselves and observe our own progress.

This could seem like a radical idea, but it's time to change that and move forward with your confidence building. Maybe you're cringing right now, but something as simple as small, achievable goals can be a great way to monitor and observe progress.

A mistake that many people make is setting goals that aren't possible – they list their dreams and aspirations which is great, but they need to recognize them as being a future dream or aspiration rather than being one goal. In reality, the bigger goals are possible, but they are so far away and before we get to it, we have so many other steps to take along the way.

The thing that we don't see, is that these steps are progress towards that dream, but they go unrecognized. We end up feeling demotivated when it comes to our goal because it's so far out of our reach, and we don't see the leaps we are taking towards it.

Eventually our goal becomes a pipe dream.

If goals are too big, we are in danger of setting ourselves up for failure. That's not to say we shouldn't have big dreams, but we need to understand that bigger goals take time, so this is not something that you're going to achieve quickly. The smaller the goal, the easier it is to track and monitor progress.

Big goals versus small goals

A great tip for goal setting is to start with a big goal or dream (this is when you can aim big) and keep breaking it down into smaller parts until you have short, achievable goals or steps that you can achieve quickly and monitor the progress. Further to this, you need to write down your goals and tick them off as you achieve each of them. This way, you can see what you've accomplished towards your end goal.

You may already be aware of ways to goal set and mark

off your progress, but the question here is, *do you give yourself credit for these achievements?*

Many people treat ticking off their goals as a kind of to-do list, and they fail to give themselves any credit at all. It's time to alter how you monitor and observe your goals from now on. Start checking your goals weekly and commend yourself on what you've achieved.

When we make a mistake, no matter how small, we always feel bad about it, right? Most people do, in fact they dwell on it and make it out to be worse than it is. Now, what about if you accomplish a small goal? *Do you praise yourself? Do you feel good? Do you treat yourself?*

If not, then how do you celebrate the win?

If you feel bad about making mistakes and you are hard on yourself as a result, but you don't celebrate your wins, then eventually your morale will be non-existent. *How long can you keep putting yourself down, without boosting yourself up?* You are on the path to destroying your confidence and it's not a good balance because if we scold ourselves when we make mistakes, we should be boosting ourselves when we accomplish something.

If you don't celebrate your wins then you are making a big mistake. We are quick to acknowledge our mistakes, but this is a negative action that can actually affect our motivation, so *why don't we celebrate our wins and boost our motivation instead?* We'd find that if we did celebrate our wins and boost our motivation more, we could be more productive in our life.

Again, this is down to the way we think because we just aren't used to being positive and celebrating our own success. Thinking in this way would in fact, give us power and it scares us – you can boost your own positivity and motivation by acknowledging and celebrating your wins.

But why?

It's because we feel energized by chemicals that are released in our brain that make us feel proud of ourselves. This encourages us to take further action, thus increasing our motivation. When we have something to be proud of, we shouldn't be ashamed. We should be shouting this from the rooftops...

> *"When you're different, sometimes you don't see the millions of people who accept you for what you are. All you notice is the person who doesn't."*
>
> Jodi Picoult, Change of Heart
> (Goodreads.com, 2020)[xxx].

We should also celebrate when we make a change or do something successfully. For example, if we want to start exercising each day and then we successfully exercise, it's an achievement. We've made a positive change in our life and we should certainly reinforce that. If we continue to reinforce wins and celebrate them, our motivation will soar and in turn this will have a positive impact on our self-esteem and confidence (Edblad, n.d.)[xxxi].

What if I don't know I've achieved something?

This notion may seem strange to some, but whether you believe it or not, because we don't celebrate our achievements, we don't always recognize them as being an something to celebrate. When confidence is low, it can be difficult for us to automatically consider that we've been triumphant. Writing it down makes it easier to monitor progress, but how can we prevent ourselves from just ticking it off our to-do list and that being the end of it? *How can we notice our own progress if we don't recognize it?* Well, this is something we can learn. We start by learning to recognize achievements and then we work on the progress monitoring and celebrations. Remember, one step at a time!

There's no doubt that every day, you accomplish or achieve something. This could be a personal goal, a work goal or even a relationship goal but regardless, we achieve it. When you're reflecting in your journal, start thinking about what you've achieved that day. This is your first step to raising your awareness and finding out just what you're capable of.

The most important part of celebrating a win is awareness and acknowledgement. This is the foundation of this whole action. We have to be able to clearly decide whether or not something was a win or not. If it's something that you've meant to do for some time, or something that will improve your life, or something you've achieved then it's a win. Next time you tick something off your list, or you do something successfully don't just brush it off. Ask yourself – *is this a win?* Make sure you open your mind and take the lead. Be strong in your own decisions and if it meets your needs, makes you smile or feel remotely happy then celebrate. Think about your win and tell someone. Push it to the front of your mind and embrace it. Celebrate it!

Recognizing accomplishments helps us to feel good and this increases our confidence. Knowing that we are not stagnant, and we are making progress can really push us and we'll be motivated to do more. It can help us improve our feelings, anxiety, and self-doubt, and it can even prompt us to overcome our shyness and be brave.

Becoming aware takes practice at first because we get stuck in negative thought patterns and we don't even realize that. We get consumed with the negative things and we don't see what is going well or the things you are good at. *We've already said that we should write down our wins, even if it's just in the form of a to-do list, but the important thing is to set aside some time each day to reflect on these and be proud.*

When we start to notice these things, the next step is to commend yourself. Once you start to see those wins, note down how you can commend them. Really appreciate them!

Recording your wins will help you to shift those negative thought patterns, because you will soon realize that although some negative things happen, the positives outweigh them. Once you train your brain to recognize the progress you've made, you can really start to celebrate your successes.

How should I celebrate my success?

Here, we are suggesting that successes should be celebrated, but many people don't bother because they don't really know how to celebrate their successes. We wouldn't feel it was warranted if we celebrated too much, but we owe it to ourselves to ensure we don't overlook or avoid the celebration too.

Sometimes, people who celebrate wins are told they are bragging. If a female entrepreneur had a great year and made mega bucks, then she disclosed this online, several people would say she was bragging. Yet big company brands such as Walmart, for example, who would've probably made at least 20 times more than the female entrepreneur, disclose their yearly profit each year but that's not viewed in the same way. Of course, I'm not saying that there are negative comments, but because it's a big company, they are required to announce this, so nobody would see this as bragging.

It's tricky to say how others should celebrate their wins

because everyone is different, and we all have different needs and expectations. There are many ways to celebrate success but if you don't know where to start, here are a few ideas:

- Treat yourself to something – this can be something small like a book, a bath bomb, a facial or beauty treatment for example. This fits in a little with self-care as we truly deserve this rewarding thing for ourselves. Self-care itself can be a fantastic reward.
- Tell your close friends or family – this can be rewarding, as it can uplift and inspire others too. Your friends and family are sure to be happy or excited for you.
- Write about it! Maybe you could write a blog post, write it in your journal, maybe even write a letter to a relevant magazine or newspaper. It's great to look back on your written pieces later.
- Why not have a win folder or collage on your laptop or in the form of a scrapbook? It's a great way to record wins. Take a picture and have a special folder to remind you of your wins. Imagery can really help you to capture and treasure those special moments.

Now, this isn't going to happen overnight so it's important to accept that, but eventually, your thought patterns will start to change and become more positive. As this happens, and you reflect more on your wins, you will begin to notice a difference in how you feel about yourself. Your mind will recognize the good and it will become automatic for you to celebrate and be proud, rather than overlook them. This will certainly turn you into a more positive person.

If you start to measure your levels of confidence in subtle ways while ensuring you embrace the experience, you will start to improve the way you feel and boost your confidence. If you record and celebrate your wins, the only way is up for you.

Confidence and self-esteem are closely linked to the way we think, feel and act. We are a complex commodity, and everything interlinks. Increasing confidence can change the way we appear on the outside as well as the inside, as others can often tell a confident person by the way they appear and act.

Days 25-27 of your 30-day Recovery Plan

JOURNALING

There's only 6 days left of your 30-day recovery plan and by now, journaling and using your journal in a reflective way will be becoming natural to you.

Over the next three days focus on your wins, no matter how big or small. Think about what you've achieved on each day – the thing that is most important to you and find a way to record it in your journal.

ACTIONABLE STEP

Write a list of things you've achieved in your life that you are proud of. This could be personal, educational or career-based achievements – anything that you are really proud of.

Our achievements often help to shape the person we are or who we become. So, keep this list, because this is a list of achievements that you may not have even celebrated yet. Reflect on your list and feel proud!

ACTIVITY

1. For your activity this time, write a list of the things you *want* to achieve in the future.
2. Turn them into a larger goal, then break them down into smaller goals if needed.
3. Pin them up in your office or keep them in the front of your journal or a diary. Something that you use on a daily basis.
4. Plan some time in your schedule to work on these goals.
5. Tick them off as you achieve them and don't forget to celebrate your wins!

Chapter 10

Establish Actions to Move Forward into a Life Exuding with Confidence

Building confidence isn't easy, it's certainly a tricky task. Once you've built it up, the hard part is over, but you still need to take measures to ensure you don't lose it (again). You need to lay your foundations and cement them, until confidence becomes second nature to you. You can then go forward and grow!

This chapter is more about maintenance. The idea is to

ensure you overcome anxiety, self-doubt and shyness, but once you've done this, you need to keep them under control. Setbacks are normal, so don't worry if you suffer a dip in your confidence or self-esteem. You can refer back to any part of this book at any time, to help you build and develop any aspect of your confidence once more.

You should certainly watch out for the warning signs we've discussed in the earlier chapters for identifying low-confidence, self-esteem and anxiety. Use your newly found knowledge to build up a keen awareness, meaning you can solve confidence issues before they dip or spiral. Awareness and prevention are key concepts here!

Retaining confidence, even if there are setbacks

Life is full of setbacks. We have ups and we have downs; that's the way it goes. When there are setbacks, it can be hard to stay positive because we are prevented from achieving what we want to achieve.

We've talked about the way we think throughout this book, and for this part, this is no exception because we need to change the way we think about setbacks. To do this, you need to build acceptance, work on your problem-solving techniques and prepare yourself to face your fears and push forward. Setbacks are not your enemy!

First of all, please remember that setbacks happen to everyone – there are no exceptions. Therefore, it's important not to take them personally. If we separate ourselves from the setback, it won't affect our confidence so heavily as we aren't connected to it. In order to separate ourselves from our setback, we need to think about it as a separate entity and really examine it, to find out what happened and where it went wrong – *what caused the setback?* We can then learn from our setbacks which can change the way we handle things in the future. *Don't forget to reflect on what you've learned from your experience and what you will do differently next time!*

If you suffer a setback, take a moment to reflect and

solve the problem. This is another way to maintain your confidence levels and if you choose to keep on with the journaling (which is highly recommended), you can talk about this in your journal and reflect later. Take a minute, and a few deep breaths before you begin. On occasions, there may be times when sleeping, breathing exercises, or meditation might help you put things back into perspective or aid you in your mission to problem-solve your issue. Try this, and if it helps, you know you can use this method effectively in the future.

Sometimes, setbacks are a little more complex, so to get over them you should write them down and brainstorm a series of solutions. Our mindset is the reason we allow these problems to get on top of us but there is a simple way to reframe this, so you can think about setbacks in a different way…

You should treat your setback as a challenge and find a way around it. It's simply a temporary barrier that you can overcome. If you solve or overcome your setback, your confidence will remain intact.

Another great way to retain your confidence is to reflect on your wins. In chapter 9, we looked at big wins and small wins, and how we can celebrate them. Reflecting on our recorded wins can really boost us when we feel low. It could also lead us to the answer we are looking for when dealing with setbacks.

Finally, take a break and do something for you. We've talked about self-care and about celebrating both wins and achievements, but what better way to retain our confidence than helping and treating ourselves?

Once you learn to overcome your setbacks, you will feel liberated.

Don't forget to set goals for your future too and give yourself something to look forward to!

Establish a daily routine that boosts your confidence and self-esteem

Get a routine – you must've had this preached to you a

thousand times, right? Well, people who have a routine for at least part of their day are often more organized and successful so if you don't have one already, read this section and do it!

A routine helps us to stay focused and organized. It prevents us from straying, and it can help us to follow our goals and monitor progress or performance. A routine instills confidence, because we never wonder what we should be doing, because we KNOW – it's part of our routine.

But make sure your routine works for you...

The most important thing about starting a new daily routine is to do what's best for you. There are some ideas of how you can start a positive daily routine below, but if something doesn't work for you, tweak it. We are all different and have our own individual needs and expectations. The road to boosting confidence involves taking ownership of your life and not being afraid to do what's best for you in the long-term.

Start by getting early. Getting up early can really set you up for the day but remember, it's still important that you get enough sleep too. So, this means that if you're a night owl, you need to go to bed earlier and ensure you get around 7-8 hours sleep. Sleep can vary among people, so this is just a guideline. Some need a little more, while others a little less.

You must stay hydrated. Drinking plenty of water is key, in order to keep you replenished. The first thing you do when you wake up should be to drink a glass of water and rehydrate your body. You should also plan your meals and healthy snacks for the day, to keep you energized.

When we first wake up, it takes our body a short time to adjust. When you open your eyes and you've had a drink, try sitting with a notebook for 10-20 minutes and write whatever comes into your brain – don't overthink it. We've talked through this technique already, but it can be really useful. This technique can be especially useful for creative people and some people choose to keep a notebook right by their bed and do this before they rehydrate.

There are a few activities you can do to get yourself off to a positive start. The most effective is some light exercise, so get out your yoga mat, take the dog for a walk, and even try some meditation. Even if you just exercise for 10-30 minutes, it's still something and it sets you on the right path for the day.

Before you start, write down three things you are thankful for or repeat three affirmations that you can relate to. Sometimes we need to remind ourselves of the positive things in our lives.

Use a diary or to-do list when you start your day. List down anything you must achieve that day, and some extra things that you want to achieve. Be realistic! Some people opt for time-blocking, and they block out parts of their day and dedicate them to certain things – exercise, dropping kids off at school, and, mealtimes for example. If you have something big to do, do it first, and then use the rest of the day to wind down from that, doing shorter tasks.

Make sure you set your boundaries. If you say you're going to relax and start to wind down by watching TV from 9 pm, then do it. It's also recommended that you take some time to reflect on your day. *Is there anything you could've done differently? Could you have responded more positively? How could you improve or change? What did you do that you're proud of?*

If you have trouble switching off, the best thing to do is to read something to help take your mind somewhere else or try journaling. Journaling can really help you to empty your mind and as you've wrote everything down, you know you won't forget it so you can relax. Journaling for around 30 minutes each evening is highly recommended.

As mentioned earlier, ensure you get enough sleep. Go to bed earlier and relax. Take a bath or use breathing or meditation techniques if required to help you settle down. Getting enough sleep really determines how we feel and perform the next day.

Many of the things we've discussed in our daily routine relate to us taking care of ourselves. We must keep our mind and body healthy and in order. That's because being in a routine, planning for productivity, and self-care make us happy and this reflects in how we think, act, and feel. If we can start to work on ourselves and process our thoughts in an effective, yet positive way, we can harness power.

This will certainly lead to high levels of confidence and self-esteem!

The final point to make now, is to explain the importance of not being harsh on yourself. Always be prepared to forgive yourself (as well as others). It's time to accept that we all make mistakes, it's human nature. It's the way we deal with these mistakes that matters.

7 Tips to bounce back faster when you make mistakes

Everyone makes mistakes, so the most effective thing

we can do is to attempt to move past them. If we make mistakes there are some things you can do to bounce back quickly.

- Accept that mistakes are normal. Nobody is perfect - everyone makes mistakes. Acceptance is key to overcoming the problem fast.
- Give yourself a break. Don't overly scorn yourself. Acknowledge the mistake and move on.
- Move on by addressing the mistake and reframing how we view this. Admit the mistake but reframe it. If you make a mistake, you are putting barriers in your own way. You need to overcome them – this is no different than any other problem in your daily life, so you need to see it that way. View your mistake as a challenge!
- Write down what you would've done differently.
- Brainstorm your problem/mistake. How can you fix or overcome this? Maybe you can work around this? Break it down into small steps and set goals.
- Review your achievements for the last week and commend yourself. Be happy and proud!
- Meditate to clear your mind and repeat your three affirmations or the three things you are thankful for.

This will help you to feel relaxed and think clearly.

Remember, everyone makes mistakes and the most important thing is to learn and move forward. We should never bury our head in the sand, we should try to bounce back, and fast. The quicker we bounce back, the less likely we are to damage our confidence.

Negative emotions and how to deal with them

When we suffer with negative emotions, we can allow them to take hold of our very being. We need to deal with them in an effective way before they take hold. There are five steps we can take to do handle these:

1. Awareness is the first step – we need to recognize our negative emotions and thought patterns.
2. When you have a negative emotion, write it down. Make a table so you can monitor these. Think about... *How are you feeling? What happened to cause this? What would you change?* When you start to investigate what caused the negative emotion, you will often realize that it isn't that bad,

and it's something that can be reframed or fixed.
3. Once you have begun to notice, record and monitor your negative emotions; you should start to unpack them. *Do you notice any patterns?*
4. The next step is to stop reacting. Next time you notice you are having a negative emotion, stop. Pause and don't react. Rethink it. Start to deal with your emotion before it shows.
5. Use some breathing exercises to cope with the initial emotion and calm your mind. It can calm you down quickly so that you don't have time to be hard on yourself. This will be less damaging to your self-esteem and it also helps you to think clearly too.

When we begin to experience negative emotions and behaviors it's important to recognize them before they escalate. Your journaling can help you identify them and then it's important to act. Just because you have one bad day, doesn't mean you're on the path to negativity so don't let this idea control which path you choose. You have to take the rough with the smooth and that's why it's important to be tough and build our resilience.

How to develop your resilience

Your resilience develops over time. Resilience is your strength within, and this is really important. It's that little feeling or voice inside that prevents us from giving up and encourages us to keep going until we get what we're striving for. If you are resilient, you can start to handle your mistakes more effectively and as a result, your stress levels will improve with practice, every day.

Confidence and resilience work together, hand in hand. You will find that you learn to control and manage your feelings, thoughts and actions better, which means your confidence grows. Problems will affect you less because you are able to spot them early on, rethink them, and focus on solutions rather than the issue. Your confidence will start to shape your personality and you will doubt yourself less. This means you will make faster decisions, more confidently.

Being resilient means you can cope with difficult situations well and you will become an action taker by tackling problems head on and leading by example. You will spend less time dwelling on problems or reacting in a negative way, as you just learn to cope and take action.

If you want to grow your resilience further, you need to develop a positive mindset. We mentioned earlier that we should aim to prevent our negative thought patterns once we are aware, but now it's time to push that even further by turning them into something positive.

Taking care of your mind and body will help to improve resilience and stamina. It's not only important to stay physically fit, you need to be mentally fit too. Keep working on yourself and take care of yourself. Staying hydrated and ensuring you eat healthily and maintaining a healthy diet can help too.

Maintaining your ideal level of confidence and self-esteem

We all have a certain ideal level of confidence and self-esteem so once we reach that, the work is done, *right?* **WRONG...**

We need to maintain this level and ensure we don't lose this again. Repeat after me, *I will not allow my confidence to be beat down again...*

Well done, you've made the pledge and that's a start, but *how can you maintain your confidence and self-esteem?*

- You can start by continuing with the self-care. Don't allow yourself to slip back into the pattern of not caring for yourself.
- Continue with the journaling. Journaling has been a major part of this whole book and this is something you should continue with.
- A daily routine is a great way to relieve stress and ensure you have balance in your life. This again will help you to maintain your ideal level of confidence and self-esteem.
- Keep your mind and body fit and healthy. Ensure you eat healthy and keep your energy levels up by eating healthy snacks. Drink plenty of water and it can also be a good idea to limit things like alcohol

and caffeine.
- Stay aware. Question yourself and ask yourself, *am I being negative?* If you notice those negative thoughts creeping up on you, you should examine and break down your thoughts again. Reprogram your thinking and deal with these.

Keeping a healthy level of confidence and self-esteem is crucial to your success. You want to maintain this and overcome the barriers for good that scupper your happiness and niggle away at your self-worth, anxieties, and imprison your braveness. You owe it to yourself, to never allow your confidence and self-esteem to dip to such a low level. You have your methods and your tips to grow your self-confidence and develop it, and therefore you have the tools you need to grow.

We welcome and applaud the new, positive and confident, you!

Days 28-30 of your 30-day Recovery Plan

JOURNAL

Well, you did it! It's your final 3 days of your 30-day recovery plan. *How did you find journaling? Was it helpful?*

In these final 3 days I want you to really think about maintaining confidence and self-esteem. Out of everything you tried, *what methods were the most effective when dealing with your confidence issues?* You should reflect on how your confidence has improved over the last 30 days, and *how your anxiety, shyness and self-worth has improved too!*

ACTIONABLE STEP

Map out a daily routine that suits you and stick to it for the next three days. Journal about it, then at the end of the three days, reflect on your experience. Remember this routine should meet your own needs and expectations!

ACTIVITY

Create a maintenance plan to keep your self-esteem and self-confidence intact. This should be fairly simple so it can be built into your routine.

Is there anything that improves your confidence or gives you a boost?
What's your favorite method of maintenance?

Make sure you try some new methods. Maybe you could attend a music or exercise class of some sort. Once you've built this into your routine and you're trying out the methods, reflect on them.

Are there any methods that worked or did not work for you?

Remember, you can amend your maintenance plan to suit your own needs.

Moving Forward…

Now you have completed your 30-day plan, you should

understand confidence, how it works and how it impacts our lives. Confidence is complex – it's a mindset, a feeling and so much more. Confidence can help to shape our personal lives, relationships, education and careers. It can be the deciding factor in what path we choose in life. Throughout this book you've learned about the causes of high and low confidence, and its impact. You've also been talked through ways of improving this and overcoming your barriers that affect your anxiety, self-doubt, and shyness.

Now that you know yourself, the maintenance steps should be fairly simple for you to follow. You have a plan of action and at any time you can refer back to any of the chapters and activities to control, monitor, and boost your confidence again.

Your next steps in your confidence journey are simple. The goals you created in the earlier chapters are possible, and you can strive for these now. Start to make a plan of action that details how you can achieve your goals. Remember, when you learn something new, you're not an expert in that topic instantly, so it can be overwhelming. Use the tools you've learned throughout this book to shape your mindset and overcome any barriers you face. Remember to celebrate the small wins as well as the big wins, as both are as equally important.

Your courage and honesty will take you a long way. You are capable of leading this journey on your own because you are confident, strong and fearless.

DID YOU ENJOY THIS BOOK?

We would truly appreciate if you could leave a review on Amazon. We are an independent publishing company and read each and every review!

amazon
★★★★★

Conclusion

There's no question that confidence is the most prominent barrier when we are trying to achieve our dreams. If we don't control it, it can control us, and once it takes hold it becomes extremely difficult to dominate it once more, and this creates a problem. If there was a confidence switch attached to our mind, then everyone would've used this at some point in their life because this is not a new concept. There are attempts to batter our confidence daily, and for some of us, we self-sabotage. That's why the 30-day recovery plan in this book is so important to help us take back control and use our confidence to our own advantage.

> *"Once we believe in ourselves, we can risk curiosity, wonder, spontaneous delight, or any experience that reveals the human spirit"*
>
> E.E. Cummings (Goodreads.com, 2020)[xxxii]

There are so many things linked to the idea of self-confidence. It links to our feelings of self-worth, self-belief, our emotions, our behavior and actions. It stems from the beliefs and ideas we hold that are embedded in us and ingrained into everything we do. While confidence can be a great thing at its height, it can also lead to a downhill struggle when it is at its lowest point. That's because the E.E. Cummings quote above is true, when we believe in ourselves, we begin to take risks because it motivates us to move forward and encourages us to develop ourselves. That's because of our confidence levels.

The aim of this book initially was to raise the readers confidence and self-esteem within 30-days, but it is so much more than that. It sends you on a journey and reminds us that everyone is different, and we move at a different pace. Not only did we examine ways to improve anxiety issues, get rid of self-doubt, and develop from shy little mice into brave and confident warriors, but the recovery plan also led us on our journey of self-discovery. It is the self-discovery that fuels this journey.

The confidence journey is complex and although the plan of this book is 30-days, you should be prepared to do further work on your confidence as some people's confidence issues run much deeper than others. Remember, confidence needs to be maintained too, so it's not something that we can fix and then it's fixed for good, it's something that we need to nurture!

Self-discovery is an important part of building self-confidence, because in order to improve or develop certain aspects of ourselves, we need to really know ourselves and that includes our triggers. Sometimes, we are forced to reflect deeper and for some people, past events are painful. The most challenging part of this plan is to work through your beliefs and reflect on what your core beliefs are and what influenced them. To understand them completely, you were asked to unpack your past. We can safely say that when we've believed with certainty in things or had certain ideas for a long period of time, it's not easy to change them. It's a working progress that challenges everything we thought we believed in, and it's often the foundations we built our values on. Everyone knows that when you mess with the foundations, the whole structure needs to be rebuilt. If you have already been working on forging new beliefs and values, you need to recognize that this is a big step that may take longer than 30-days, although if you follow this book closely, you should certainly experience improvements over this time. Don't worry about this, just take one step at a time.

This book focuses a lot on building awareness and while this concept can be so simple, it's priceless when it comes to confidence. Awareness is key as we must realize what barriers stand in the way of our future. This book looks at a range of issues that are brought to light through a lack of confidence, including relationships, careers, education, and our personal life. There's no doubt that we need to be aware of when and why our confidence is low, as well as how to boost it. While nothing can stop a confidence dip, the strategies and tools have ensured we are able to overcome it, without it spiraling out of control.

Self-care is growing in popularity and everywhere we turn, people are focusing on this lately. Self-care is important, and it is known to reduce stress levels and feelings of depression. It's also amazing how much self-care relates to everything to do with the 'self' that we have covered throughout this book. Self-care has an impact on our self-belief, self-worth, self-esteem, self-doubt and most of all, our self-confidence. The whole idea of one's 'self' and the care or nurturing we provide to our self is often the driving force of everything as it's all connected. If we do not feel self-worth, we may reduce our level of self-care, but this just increases that feeling of worthlessness, and eventually affects our self-esteem, self-belief. This can then bring down our self-belief and each of these chip away at our confidence levels. These continue to reduce until we do something to stop it or it's reduced to an all-time low. As we've uncovered throughout this book, this can lead to further stress and depression, as well as other mental health issues.

Now that you've followed the 30-day Recovery Plan your self-confidence should have improved and you should be in a routine that includes self-care and journaling, and your self-confidence should be at a nice level.

Congratulations on your achievement, you've made fantastic progress!

As you know, that's not the end, but the beginning of your journey because now the maintenance begins and now you can strive for those dreams you've always wanted to achieve but have felt unable to push for. If you keep working on your self-confidence and use the tools that you've learned in this book to overcome your anxieties, your shyness and self-doubt, the world is yours and opportunities will arise! It's time to use your confidence and grab your dreams with both hands.

Can you hear it now?

Hello, it's *your* confidence calling!

Reference List

[i] Wolfgang von Goethe, J. (2019). *Self Confidence Quotes (1298 quotes)*. [online] Goodreads.com. Available at: https://www.goodreads.com/quotes/tag/self-confidence [Accessed 27 Nov. 2019].

[ii] Goodreads.com. (2020). *Self Confidence Quotes (1311 quotes)*. [online] Available at: https://www.goodreads.com/quotes/tag/self-confidence [Accessed 13 Jan. 2020].

[iii] Segal, Peter (2003). *Anger Management*. Columbia Pictures. USA. https://en.wikipedia.org/wiki/Anger_Management_(film) [accessed 11 Jan. 2020]

[iv] Roosevelt, T. (2019). *Self Confidence Quotes (1298 quotes)*. [online] Goodreads.com. Available at: https://www.goodreads.com/quotes/tag/self-confidence [Accessed 27 Nov. 2019].

[v] PositivePsychology.com. (2019). *What is Self-Confidence? + 9 Ways to Increase It [2019 Update]*. [online] Available at: https://positivepsychology.com/self-confidence/ [Accessed 27

Nov. 2019].

[vi] Verywell Mind. (2020). *How Self-Actualized People Frequently Have Their Needs Met.* [online] Available at: https://www.verywellmind.com/characteristics-of-self-actualized-people-2795963 [Accessed 16 Jan. 2020].

[vii] Lifehack. (2020). *10 Warning Signs of Low Self-Esteem and a Lack of Confidence.* [online] Available at: https://www.lifehack.org/articles/communication/10-warning-signs-that-you-have-low-self-confidence.html [Accessed 20 Jan. 2020].

[viii] Mcleod, S. (2012). *Low Self Esteem | Simply Psychology.* [online] Simplypsychology.org. Available at: https://www.simplypsychology.org/self-esteem.html [Accessed 7 Dec. 2019].

[ix] Psychology Today. (2018). *5 Reasons People Have Low Self-Confidence.* [online] Available at: https://www.psychologytoday.com/us/blog/shyness-is-nice/201812/5-reasons-people-have-low-self-confidence [Accessed 9 Dec. 2019].

[x] Onoda, K., Okamoto, Y., Nakashima, K., Nittono, H., Yoshimura, S., Yamawaki, S., Yamaguchi, S. and Ura, M. (2010). *Volume 5 Issue 4 December 2010 Article Contents Abstract METHODS RESULTS DISCUSSION REFERENCES < Previous Next > pdfPDF Split ViewCite Permissions Icon Permissions Share Does low self-esteem enhance social pain? The relationship between trait self-esteem and anterior cingulate cortex activation induced by ostracism.* [online] Available at: https://academic.oup.com/scan/article/5/4/385/1623198 [Accessed 9 Dec. 2019].

[xi] Psychology Today. (2018). *5 Reasons People Have Low Self-Confidence.* [online] Available at: https://www.psychologytoday.com/us/blog/shyness-is-nice/201812/5-reasons-people-have-low-self-confidence [Accessed 9 Dec. 2019].

[xii] Counselling-directory.org.uk. (2016). *Identifying low self-esteem thoughts and behaviours.* [online] Available at:

https://www.counselling-directory.org.uk/memberarticles/identifying-low-self-esteem-thoughts-and-behaviours [Accessed 9 Dec. 2019].

[xiii] Counselling-directory.org.uk. (2016). *Identifying low self-esteem thoughts and behaviours.* [online] Available at: https://www.counselling-directory.org.uk/memberarticles/identifying-low-self-esteem-thoughts-and-behaviours [Accessed 9 Dec. 2019].

[xiv] Counselling-directory.org.uk. (2016). *Identifying low self-esteem thoughts and behaviours.* [online] Available at: https://www.counselling-directory.org.uk/memberarticles/identifying-low-self-esteem-thoughts-and-behaviours [Accessed 9 Dec. 2019].

[xv] Counselling-directory.org.uk. (2016). *Identifying low self-esteem thoughts and behaviours.* [online] Available at: https://www.counselling-directory.org.uk/memberarticles/identifying-low-self-esteem-thoughts-and-behaviours [Accessed 9 Dec. 2019].

[xvi] Counselling-directory.org.uk. (2016). *Identifying low self-esteem thoughts and behaviours.* [online] Available at: https://www.counselling-directory.org.uk/memberarticles/identifying-low-self-esteem-thoughts-and-behaviours [Accessed 9 Dec. 2019].

[xvii] Counselling-directory.org.uk. (2016). *Identifying low self-esteem thoughts and behaviours.* [online] Available at: https://www.counselling-directory.org.uk/memberarticles/identifying-low-self-esteem-thoughts-and-behaviours [Accessed 9 Dec. 2019].

[xviii] Curtin, M. (2018). *Are You Shy or Introverted? Science Says This Is the Difference Between Them.* [online] Inc.com. Available at: https://www.inc.com/melanie-curtin/are-you-shy-or-introverted-science-says-this-is-1-primary-difference.html [Accessed 12 Dec. 2019].

[xix] Introvert, Dear. (2019). *Introvert / Extrovert Test: This Simple Quiz Reveals Which One You Are.* [online] Available at: https://in-

trovertdear.com/introvert-extrovert-test-quiz/ [Accessed 15 Dec. 2019].

[xx] Goodreads.com. (2020). *Self Confidence Quotes (1311 quotes)*. [online] Available at: https://www.goodreads.com/quotes/tag/self-confidence [Accessed 13 Jan. 2020].

[xxi] Impostor Syndrome. (2020). *Everyone loses when bright people play small*. [online] Available at: https://impostorsyndrome.com/unpacking-michelle-obamas-impostor-syndrome/ [Accessed 20 Jan. 2020].

[xxii] Dalla-Camina, M. (2018). *The Reality of Imposter Syndrome*. [online] Psychology Today. Available at: https://www.psychologytoday.com/us/blog/real-women/201809/the-reality-imposter-syndrome [Accessed 15 Dec. 2019].

[xxiii] Healthline. (n.d.). *11 Signs and Symptoms of Anxiety Disorders*. [online] Available at: https://www.healthline.com/nutrition/anxiety-disorder-symptoms#section1 [Accessed 20 Dec. 2019].

[xxiv] Lifehack. (n.d.). *15 Simple Ways To Get Confidence Back*. [online] Available at: https://www.lifehack.org/articles/communication/15-simple-ways-get-confidence-back.html [Accessed 19 Dec. 2019].

[xxv] AGATHANGELOU, F. (2015). *Stop Comparing Yourself to Others to Improve Self-Esteem | HealthyPlace*. [online] Healthyplace.com. Available at: https://www.healthyplace.com/blogs/buildingselfesteem/2015/05/how-to-stop-comparing-yourself-to-others [Accessed 22 Dec. 2019].

[xxvi] Petersen, N. (2017). *The Dangers of Comparing Yourself to Others on Social Media | AllPsych Blog*. [online] AllPsych Blog. Available at: https://blog.allpsych.com/the-dangers-of-comparing-yourself-to-others-on-social-media/ [Accessed 22 Dec. 2019].

[xxvii] Bokhari, D. (2019). *You Are NOT Your Inner Dialogue*. [online] Meaningfulhq.com. Available at: https://www.meaningfulhq.com/you-are-not-your-inner-

dialogue.html [Accessed 24 Dec. 2019].

[xxviii] Ackerman, C. (2019). *What is Self-Worth and How Do We Increase it? (Incl. 4 Worksheets).* [online] PositivePsychology.com. Available at: https://positivepsychology.com/self-worth/ [Accessed 3 Jan. 2020].

[xxix] Ackerman, C. (2019). *What is Self-Worth and How Do We Increase it? (Incl. 4 Worksheets).* [online] PositivePsychology.com. Available at: https://positivepsychology.com/self-worth/ [Accessed 3 Jan. 2020].

[xxx] Goodreads.com. (2020). *Self Confidence Quotes (1311 quotes).* [online] Available at: https://www.goodreads.com/quotes/tag/self-confidence [Accessed 13 Jan. 2020].

[xxxi] Edblad, P. (n.d.). *The Power of Small Wins: Why Celebrating Your Progress is Crucial for Long-Term Success – Patrik Edblad.* [online] Patrik Edblad. Available at: https://patrikedblad.com/self-discipline/the-power-of-small-wins/ [Accessed 6 Jan. 2020].

[xxxii] Goodreads.com. (2020). *Self Confidence Quotes (1311 quotes).* [online] Available at: https://www.goodreads.com/quotes/tag/self-confidence [Accessed 13 Jan. 2020].

www.ingramcontent.com/pod-product-compliance
Lightning Source LLC
Chambersburg PA
CBHW020859080526
44589CB00011B/364